Praise from the Expert

"Finally! An answer to my students' questions about recommended JSL books!

"This book contains exactly the kind of simple examples I have been looking to recommend to my students interested in JSL scripting. It breaks down the learning into understandable pieces, with examples. It starts off with exactly the same JSL topics that I start with curious students.

"To my surprise, this book also contains the next step to my personal JSL learning."

Diana Ballard
Consulting Statistician, Artemis

"For the first-time JMP scripter, the book provides an efficient introduction to JMP scripting and a wealth of examples to assist with the assimilation of all of the capabilities of JMP scripting. The book may be even more valuable to the experienced JMP scripter. The "How To" section of the book, which from a page count perspective comprises about two-thirds of the book, provides examples that are extremely valuable in making one's scripts quick to produce and efficient in processing.

"Anyone who wants to become a serious JMP scripter or considers themselves a serious JMP scripter should have a copy of this book."

Jim Nelson
Manager,
FSL/IT/CIM/Yield Management Systems

"*Jump into JMP® Scripting* is an excellent book for beginner JMP scripters. It is a nice complement to the *JMP® Scripting Guide* and help files. It contains detailed examples, complete with code snippets, log entries, and screen shots. The authors show examples of code that don't work and those that do. They have worked in JMP tech support for many years, they know what scripters struggle with, and they have answered many common beginner questions in this book. Reading this book is like having tech support standing beside you as you venture into JSL."

Diane K. Michelson
SEMATECH

Jump into JMP® Scripting

Wendy Murphrey

Rosemary Lucas

The correct bibliographic citation for this manual is as follows: Murphrey, Wendy, and Rosemary Lucas. *Jump into JMP® Scripting.* Cary, NC: SAS Institute Inc.

Jump into JMP® Scripting

Copyright © 2009, SAS Institute Inc., Cary, NC, USA

ISBN 978-1-59994-658-0

SAS Institute Inc., SAS Campus Drive, Cary, North Carolina 27513.

1st printing, August 2009

SAS® Publishing provides a complete selection of books and electronic products to help customers use SAS software to its fullest potential. For more information about our e-books, e-learning products, CDs, and hard-copy books, visit the SAS Publishing Web site at **support.sas.com/publishing** or call 1-800-727-3228.

Contents

Acknowledgments

Writing a book requires not only an author, but a whole host of support from many sources. In our case, one very important source of encouragement and support came from our mentor and colleague, Ryan Gilmore. Not only did Ryan teach both of us JMP Scripting Language when we started working in JMP Technical Support years ago, he critiqued this book while in its infancy and helped guide us to write a better book. Thank you, Ryan.

We would also like to thank former and present members of the JMP Technical Support team for their support, including our managers Eddie Routten and Duane Hayes. Thank you all for your encouragement.

To John Sall who conceived and started JMP software, we are inspired by your enthusiasm and honored to have the opportunity to work with you and the rest of the JMP Division.

Special thanks go to our reviewers extraordinaire, who offered their expertise and advice on our drafts despite full-time duties elsewhere: Mark Bailey, Lee Creighton, Michael Crotty, Melanie Drake, Xan Gregg, Win LeDinh, Paul Marovich, Tonya Mauldin, and Joseph Morgan.

Thank you, Stephenie Joyner, our exceptional acquisitions editor. Your sense of humor and support made the journey easier. Many thanks go to Mary Beth Steinbach, Patrice Cherry, Candy Farrell, and Jennifer Dilley, who took our drafts and created the beautiful, finished product. To Stacey Hamilton and Shelly Goodin, thanks for promoting and marketing our book. And to Julie Platt, SAS Press Editor-in-Chief, we thank you for giving us the opportunity to publish our scripting book.

And finally, we thank our families for their endless support during the writing of this book. Thank you Trey Lucas for your assistance with home computer issues and Firmin and Caroline Lucas for your support from afar. Thank you Graham and Walker Murphrey, for your patience and understanding—Yes, Mommy is finally finished with the book! And, last but not least, we especially thank our spouses, Bob Lucas and Britt Murphrey, for taking on extra duties so we could work on the book.

About This Book

Purpose

This book shows how to get started using JMP scripting language (JSL). It also provides a rich source of example scripts for those who need to accomplish a specific task with scripting.

Is This Book for You?

If you want to automate JMP analyses that you perform on a regular basis, want to know more about customizing your JMP reports, or seek a good source for example scripts, this book is for you.

Prerequisites

This book assumes that you have experience using JMP interactively and are familiar with the JMP menus and toolbars.

Scope of This Book

If you do not know anything about JSL and need to get a quick start, the first section of this book will show you how to capture scripts that JMP generates and pull these scripts together into a cohesive program.

If you do know a bit about scripting and seek examples on performing specific tasks, the second section of this book will provide you with a diverse resource of example scripts.

This book does not provide a comprehensive treatment of JSL syntax. For that information, we recommend that you consult the *JMP Scripting Guide* or the Help Indexes within the JMP software.

How This Book Is Organized

This book is divided into two main parts:

Section 1: Introduction to JSL

> **Chapter One:** Make JMP Work for You: Harnessing the Power of Scripts Generated by JMP
>
> **Chapter Two:** Stitching It Together
>
> **Chapter Three:** The Double-Layer Cake
>
> **Chapter Four:** Close Your Eyes and Jump!

Section 2: Jump On!

> **Chapter Five:** Rows, Columns, and Tables
>
> **Chapter Six:** Dialog Windows
>
> **Chapter Seven:** Analyses
>
> **Chapter Eight:** Graph Axes
>
> **Chapter Nine:** Reports and Journals

Typographical Conventions Used in This Book

The following typographic conventions are used in this book:

regular	is used for most text.
italic	*is used for emphasis and object references within text.*
bold	identifies JMP menu and dialog choices and JSL functions. Choices such as **Help ▶ About JMP** mean you select **Help**, and then select **About JMP**.
//	identifies comments within the code.
/* */	delimits lengthy comments within the code.

 Interspersed in the chapters are helpful hints, which are denoted with the shaded gray background and the chair icon. So when you see the chair icon, hold onto your seat because something important is noted here.

Software Used for This Book

JMP 8.0.1 for Windows was used to develop the scripts and create the screen shots used in this book. The scripts were also tested in JMP 6.0.3 and JMP 7.0.2, and optional scripts for these earlier releases are provided for appropriate cases in Section 2.

Many of the tables found in the JMP 8.0.1 Sample Data directory have embedded scripts, which also serve as excellent examples.

References

SAS Institute Inc. 2008. *JMP® 8 Scripting Guide*. Cary, NC: SAS Institute Inc.

SAS Institute Inc. 2008. *JMP® 8 User Guide*. Cary, NC: SAS Institute Inc.

How to Use This Book

If you know very little about scripting, then read Section 1 to get started.

If you are familiar with scripting and need to find an example for a specific scripting task, proceed to Section 2.

You will need access to JMP to work through the examples.

Author Pages

Each SAS Press author has an author's page at http://support.sas.com/publishing/authors. From the index page, select the name of the author that you are interested in and you'll find all kinds of interesting information including sneak previews of sample chapters and upcoming projects, podcast interviews, SAS tips, speaking engagements, blogs, free sample code, and more.

To access the example programs for this book, go to http://support.sas.com/jumpintojmp, and then select Example Code and Data.

For an alphabetical listing of all books for which example code is available, see http://support.sas.com/bookcode. Select a title to display the book's example code.

If you are unable to access the code through the Web site, send e-mail to **saspress@sas.com**.

Additional Resources

SAS offers you a rich variety of resources to help build your JMP skills and explore and apply the full power of JMP software. Whether you are in a professional or academic setting, we have learning products that can help you maximize your investment in JMP.

Bookstore	http://support.sas.com/publishing/
Training	http://www.jmp.com/training/
SAS Certification	http://support.sas.com/certify/
Higher Education Resources	http://support.sas.com/learn/he/
SAS OnDemand for Academics	http://support.sas.com/ondemand/

And

JMP Knowledge Base	http://www.jmp.com/forms/knowledge_base.shtml
JMP Technical Support	http://www.jmp.com/support/
Learning Center	http://support.sas.com/learn/
JMP User Community	http://www.jmp.com/community/

Comments or Questions?

If you have comments or questions about this book, you may contact the authors through SAS as follows:

Mail:

SAS Institute Inc.
SAS Press
Attn: Wendy Murphrey and Rosemary Lucas
SAS Campus Drive
Cary, NC 27513

E-mail: saspress@sas.com

Fax: (919) 677-4444

Please include the title of the book in your correspondence.

For a complete list of books available through SAS Press, visit http://support.sas.com/publishing.

SAS Publishing News: Receive up-to-date information about all new SAS publications via e-mail by subscribing to the SAS Publishing News monthly eNewsletter. Visit http://support.sas.com/subscribe.

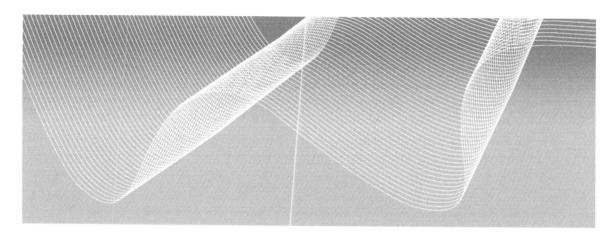

Section 1

Introduction to JSL

What is JSL? Beginning with the release of JMP 4 in 2000, a scripting language became a key feature of the software. The JMP scripting language, known as JSL, is made up of various commands that, when put together appropriately, instruct JMP to perform designated tasks automatically.

What is a JSL script? A JSL script is a program that includes a series of JSL commands that process various tasks during a single execution. JSL offers you the freedom to create scripts from the very simple and specific to the most generic and complex.

Some examples of actions that can be scripted are:

- Opening a data table
- Adding columns
- Selecting rows
- Creating subset or summary tables
- Performing various analyses
- Saving data tables, journals, and more

This list is by no means exhaustive. In fact, it is only the beginning.

 It might be best to ignore all thoughts of other programming languages that you are familiar with, because JSL is quite distinctive. Please don't try to figure out what language it is similar to at this point, as it might cause unnecessary frustration and headaches!

Chapter One

Make JMP Work for You: Harnessing the Power of Scripts Generated by JMP

Overview

Have you ever worried that you will have to write pages and pages of code, and won't know where to start? There's no need to fret, because JMP, the best scripter of all, can write the scripts for you. We're going to show you how.

In this chapter, you will learn about:

- Capturing scripts from your analyses
- Using scripts from text import
- Creating a combined script composed of two separate captured scripts

Capturing Scripts from Your Analyses

You just created a report that impresses your manager. He likes it so much that he wants the report weekly. So, what to do?

Do not panic. Instead, save the scripts and execute them next week to create your report.

In your report, you might have noticed the red triangle icons, clicked on a few of the icons, and used some of the options in the drop-down menus to add or subtract portions of your analysis. See Figure 1.1 for an example.

Figure 1.1 Bivariate Menu

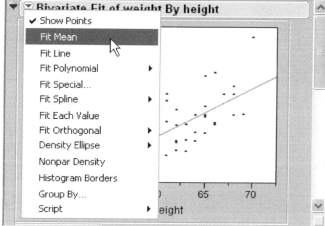

Did you know that you can capture a script of your analysis, plus many of the post-analysis changes you made? While JMP does not record every step you perform interactively, you can reproduce your results with scripting.

In Figure 1.2, notice the last item on the menu is **Script**. Selecting it opens a sub-menu that itemizes choices for saving the analysis script to regenerate the report, including most options.

Scripts that are generated by JMP can be captured in a variety of ways using selections in the **Script** menu.

Figure 1.2 Script Menu

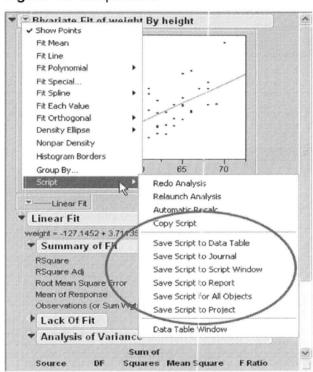

Let's take a look at three of these options.

Copying Scripts

This is an easy one. The **Copy Script** option places the script on the clipboard, and then you can paste the script wherever you need it.

Saving Scripts to a Data Table

Keeping a script with its associated data is a good idea. The **Save Script to Data Table** command stores the script as a property of the data table. As a table property/script, it stays with the table until you delete it. You can add data to the table, execute the script, and see the results. And, when you save the table you also save the script. So when you give the data table to a colleague, she can open the table, execute the scripts with the data you intended, and view your reports.

A red triangle icon is created in the table panel and is labeled with the analysis name. Clicking on the icon opens a menu with three items: **Run Script**, **Edit**, and **Delete**.

Figure 1.3 Script Property Options

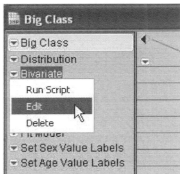

Choosing **Run Script** executes the script.

Selecting **Edit** opens a window where you can view and edit the script.

Figure 1.4 Sample Script That Was Saved as a Table Property/Script

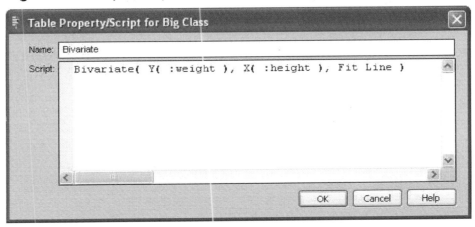

Selecting **Delete** removes the script as a table property.

 Did you know that many of the sample data tables in your JMP installation include scripts that have already been saved? Click on the red triangle icon to the left of a script that interests you, then select **Edit**, and you'll see a ready-made script.

Figure 1.5 Table Panel with Saved Scripts

Sample Scripts

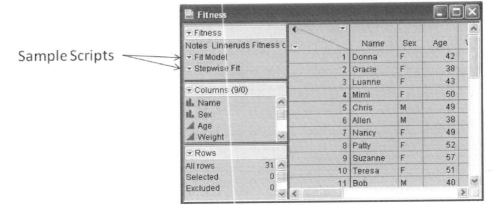

Saving Scripts to a Script Window

The **Save Script to Script Window** option places your script into a window named *Script Window*. This window is a script editor where you can edit your saved script. If this window is kept open, you can accumulate scripts from additional analyses by issuing the **Save Script to Script Window** command from those reports.

It is easy to save your script as a script file from this window. Select **File ▶ Save As**, and then select **Save As Type, JMP Scripts (*.jsl)**.

Figure 1.6 Script Window with Bivariate Script

```
Bivariate( Y( :weight ), X( :height ), Fit Line( {Line Color( "Red" )} ) );
```

Using Scripts from Text Import

When you open a text file as a data table, an import script named **Source** is added as a table property.

Figure 1.7 Text Import Table

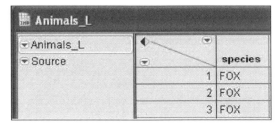

Click on the red triangle icon, and select **Edit** to see the code that JMP generated to reproduce the import of the text file. Note that the code consists of an **Open** statement with all possible settings needed to import the file.

Figure 1.8 Source Script for Text Import

```
Table Property/Script for Animals_L                                          [X]

Name:  Source

Script:  Open(
             "C:\Program Files\SAS\JMP\8\Support Files English\Sample Import Data\Animals_L.txt",
             columns(
                 species = Character,
                 subject = Numeric,
                 miles = Numeric,
                 season = Character
             ),
             Import Settings(
                 End Of Line( CRLF, CR, LF ),
                 End Of Field( Tab ),
                 Strip Quotes( 1 ),
                 Use Apostrophe as Quotation Mark( 0 ),
                 Scan Whole File( 1 ),
                 Labels( 1 ),
                 Column Names Start( 1 ),
                 Data Starts( 2 ),
                 Lines To Read( All ),
                 Year Rule( "10-90" )
             )
         )

                                          [ OK ]  [ Cancel ]  [ Help ]
```

Creating a Combined Script Composed of Two Separate Captured Scripts

Now that you've seen how easy it is to capture scripts, we are going to show you something a little more interesting. Remember that your manager wants the report generated each week? We will show you how easy it is to create a script that imports the data *and* makes the report.

In this sample, we put together a script that

- Imports the text data
- Creates a Distribution analysis

Importing the Text Data

Let's begin by importing the Bigclass_L.txt file.

1. Select **File ▶ Open**. You can find this file in the Sample Import Data folder. For a typical JMP 8 Windows installation, you would find the file here:

    C:\Program Files\SAS\JMP\8\Support Files English\Sample Import Data

    Bigclass_L.txt is a tab-delimited file. If you use the **Data, using Text Import Preferences** option as shown in Figure 1.9, tab must be specified as an End of Field option in your text import preferences.

Figure 1.9 Open Text File for Windows

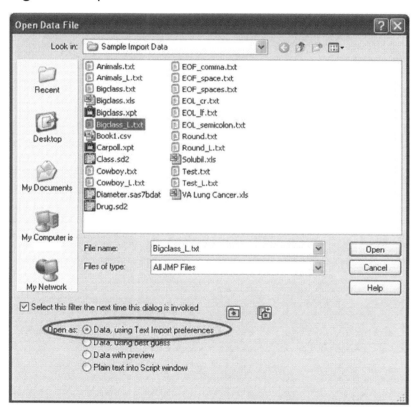

2. After the data is imported into JMP, click the red triangle icon beside **Source** and select **Edit**.

Figure 1.10 Editing the Source Script

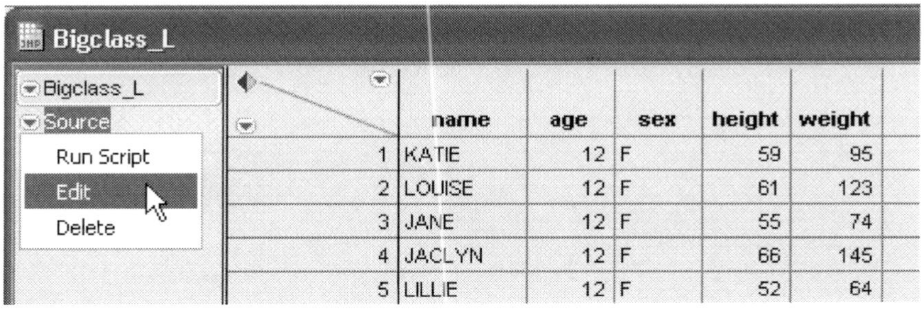

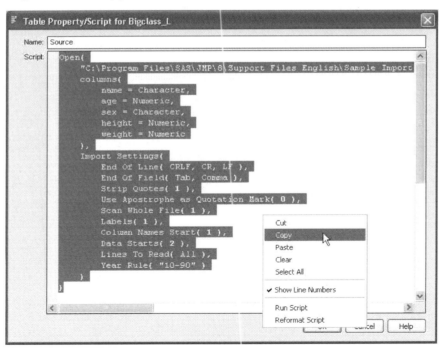

3. In the resulting window, select the entire script and copy it by right-clicking the selected text and selecting **Copy**.

Figure 1.11 Copy of Source Script

4. Click **OK** to dismiss the Source Table Script window.

5. From the **File** menu, select **New ▶ Script**.

6. Paste the script by clicking the **Edit** menu and selecting **Paste**.

7. Add a semicolon after the last closing parenthesis, because you will be adding more code.

 The semicolon, known as the **Glue** operator, is necessary in this case because it tells JMP to expect further JSL statements. Additional details about the **Glue** operator can be found in the *JMP Scripting Guide*.

Figure 1.12 Paste of Import Code

```
Script
Open(
    "C:\Program Files\SAS\JMP\8\Support Files English\Sample Import Data\Bigclass_L.txt",
    columns(
        name = Character,
        age = Numeric,
        sex = Character,
        height = Numeric,
        weight = Numeric
    ),
    Import Settings(
        End Of Line( CRLF, CR, LF ),
        End Of Field( Tab ),
        Strip Quotes( 1 ),
        Use Apostrophe as Quotation Mark( 0 ),
        Scan Whole File( 1 ),
        Labels( 1 ),
        Column Names Start( 1 ),
        Data Starts( 2 ),
        Lines To Read( All ),
        Year Rule( "10-90" )
    )
); ←
```

8. Press the **Enter** key a couple of times to move the cursor down a few lines.

Creating a Distribution Analysis

So far, we have pasted the script to import a text file into a Script window. Now, we will create a Distribution analysis and save its script.

1. From the **Analyze** menu, select **Distribution**.

2. Cast **age** in the **Y, Columns** role and click **OK**.

Figure 1.13 Distribution Dialog Window

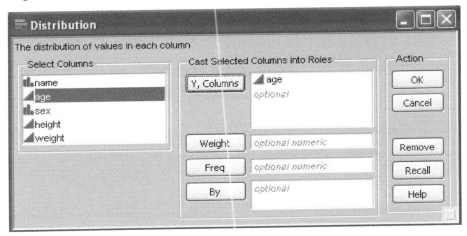

3. In the Distribution analysis window, capture the script by clicking the uppermost red triangle and selecting **Script ▶ Copy Script.**

Figure 1.14 Copy Script to Clipboard

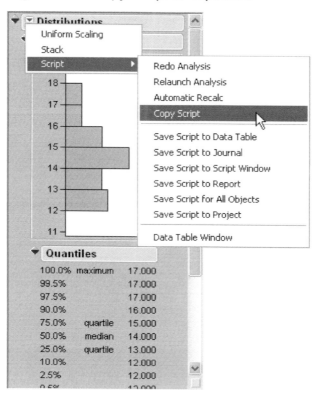

This action saves the Distribution script onto the clipboard.

Now return to the script window that contains the text import script, and place the cursor in the space below the semicolon, near the bottom of the window.

Figure 1.15 Placing the Cursor

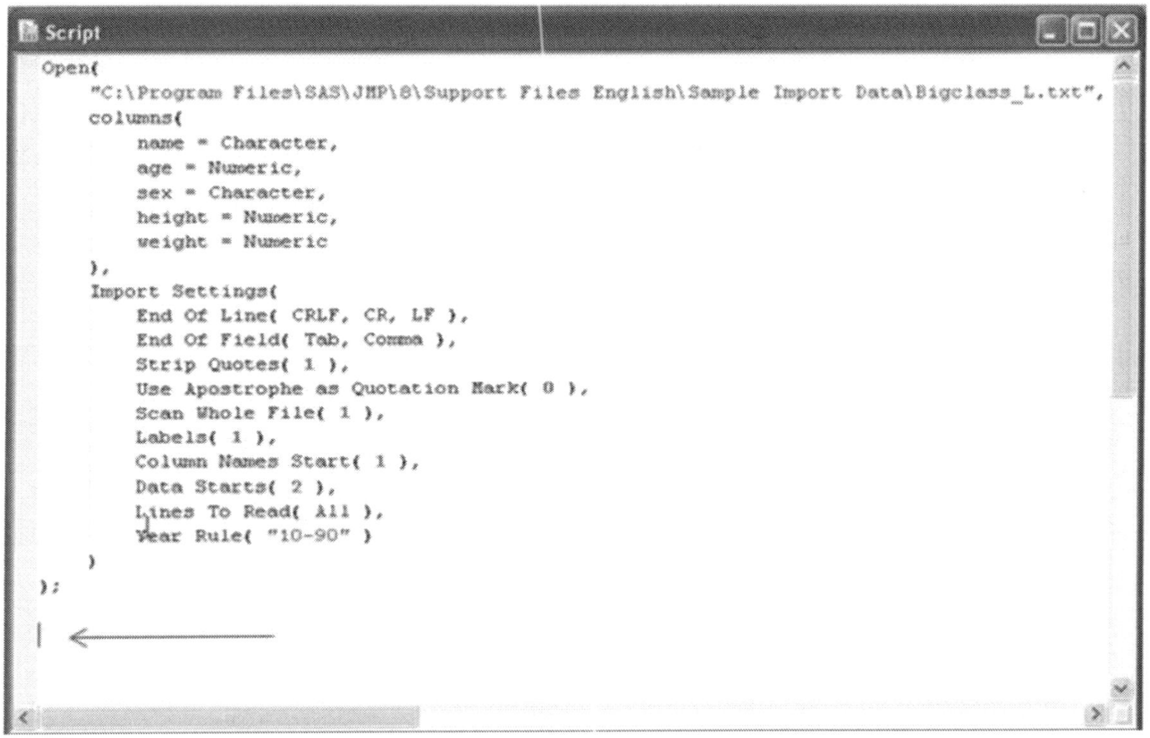

```
Script                                                                    _ □ ✕
Open(
    "C:\Program Files\SAS\JMP\8\Support Files English\Sample Import Data\Bigclass_L.txt",
    columns(
        name = Character,
        age = Numeric,
        sex = Character,
        height = Numeric,
        weight = Numeric
    ),
    Import Settings(
        End Of Line( CRLF, CR, LF ),
        End Of Field( Tab, Comma ),
        Strip Quotes( 1 ),
        Use Apostrophe as Quotation Mark( 0 ),
        Scan Whole File( 1 ),
        Labels( 1 ),
        Column Names Start( 1 ),
        Data Starts( 2 ),
        Lines To Read( All ),
        Year Rule( "10-90" )
    )
);

|  ←————————————————————
```

4. To paste the Distribution script from the clipboard into the Script window, select **Edit ▶ Paste**.

5. Add a semicolon after the last closing parenthesis in case you later decide to add code, and because this is a good programming practice.

Figure 1.16 Script Window with Distribution Script Pasted

```
Script
Open(
    "C:\Program Files\SAS\JMP\8\Support Files English\Sample Import Data\Bigclass_L.txt",
    columns(
        name = Character,
        age = Numeric,
        sex = Character,
        height = Numeric,
        weight = Numeric
    ),
    Import Settings(
        End Of Line( CRLF, CR, LF ),
        End Of Field( Tab ),
        Strip Quotes( 1 ),
        Use Apostrophe as Quotation Mark( 0 ),
        Scan Whole File( 1 ),
        Labels( 1 ),
        Column Names Start( 1 ),
        Data Starts( 2 ),
        Lines To Read( All ),
        Year Rule( "10-90" )
    )
);

Distribution( Continuous Distribution( Column( :age ) ) );  ⟵——————————
```

6. Close the Distribution analysis window we created interactively, and then close the data table, Bigclass_L, leaving the Script window open.

Finally, let's look at the different methods we can use to initiate script execution and run the script to verify that it produces the expected results.

Executing a Script

There are several ways to execute a JSL script:

- From the **Edit** menu, select **Run Script**.
- Click the **Run Script** button on the toolbar.
- Right-click anywhere in the Script Editor window, and select **Run Script** from the pop-up menu.
- Use the keyboard shortcut for this same action: **CTRL+R**.
- Double-click a JSL file from a file browser.

To *execute* or *run* a script means the same thing, and we might use the terms interchangeably throughout this book.

For this case, we will use the first method. From the **Edit** menu, select **Run Script**.

Now you will see the text imported into a data table, and the Distribution analysis executed on that data.

Figure 1.17 Results of Executing Combined Captured Scripts

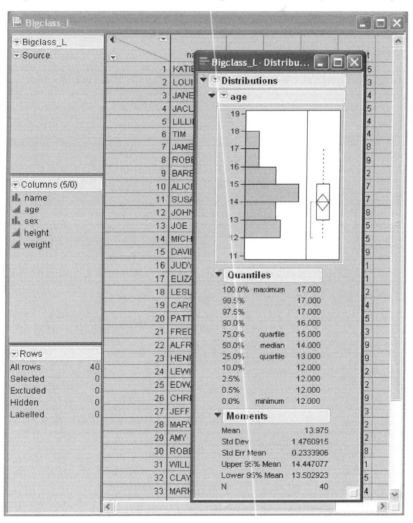

Checking the Log

The Log window is where the code that you executed is displayed, along with any messages JMP has returned. If you have not already done so, display the Log window by clicking the **View** menu, and then select **Log**.

You can either leave the Log window docked at the bottom of your JMP window so that it is always in view, or you can allow it to float, like most of the other windows inside JMP. To float the Log window, right-click anywhere inside the log, and then select **Float Log Window**.

The Log window is also a Script Editor, which means that you can select code and execute it directly from within the log.

If your Log window was open prior to executing your script, you will see the script echoed in the log.

Figure 1.18 Log Window Showing Code

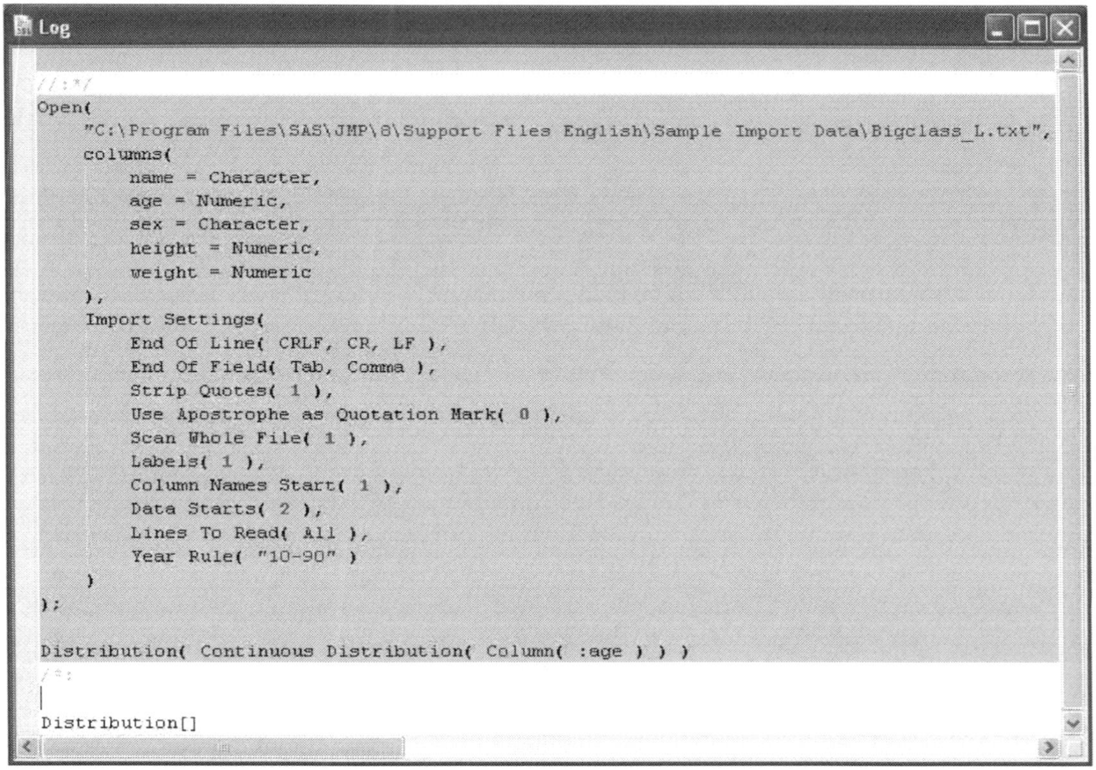

```
//:*/
Open(
    "C:\Program Files\SAS\JMP\8\Support Files English\Sample Import Data\Bigclass_L.txt",
    columns(
        name = Character,
        age = Numeric,
        sex = Character,
        height = Numeric,
        weight = Numeric
    ),
    Import Settings(
        End Of Line( CRLF, CR, LF ),
        End Of Field( Tab, Comma ),
        Strip Quotes( 1 ),
        Use Apostrophe as Quotation Mark( 0 ),
        Scan Whole File( 1 ),
        Labels( 1 ),
        Column Names Start( 1 ),
        Data Starts( 2 ),
        Lines To Read( All ),
        Year Rule( "10-90" )
    )
);

Distribution( Continuous Distribution( Column( :age ) ) )
/*:

Distribution[]
```

Saving a Script

Let's save the script because we will be coming back to it later.

1. Bring the script that we created to the forefront of the JMP application by selecting **Window ▶ Script**.

2. On the **File** menu, select **Save As**.

3. Browse to a convenient, yet memorable, location and name the script **Sample1.JSL.**

4. Click the **Save** button.

Figure 1.19 Save Sample1.JSL

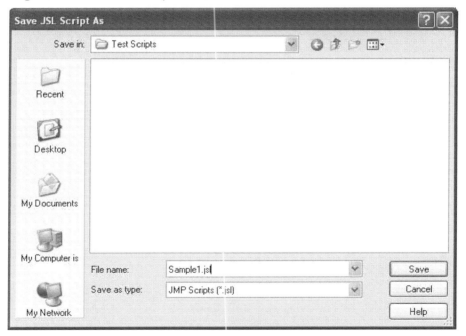

You are finished! You have put together an entire script that will

- Import text data
- Create a Distribution report

Summary

Now you've learned how JMP can work for you by creating scripts of your reports and for your imported data.

What's next? It's time to roll up your sleeves, because in the next chapter we will show you how to stitch together multiple scripts using the Script Editor.

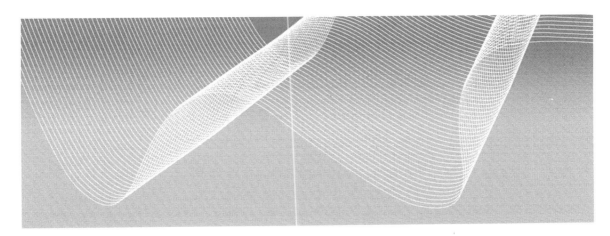

Chapter Two

Stitching It Together

Overview

After reading Chapter One, you should know how to get scripts from JMP and combine them into a single Script window. In this chapter, we will show you how to stitch the individual scripts together so that a single script will complete a variety of tasks for you at the click of a button.

In this chapter, you will learn about:

- Stitching together a Summary table and one analysis
- Stitching together the import of text data, a Summary table, and two analyses
- Creating a custom toolbar button that will execute a script

Stitching All the Scripts Together

Your manager is thrilled with the information that you have been giving him. Now, in addition to what you have already been producing weekly, he wants the data summarized, along with some further analysis.

In the previous chapter, you learned how to make JMP write the scripts for you. You also learned how to put two independent scripts together so they are executed consecutively.

Now, we will continue to show you how easy it is to combine multiple scripts; only this time, you will have to do a small amount of coding to ensure the scripts will run together successfully.

Stitching Together a Summary Table and One Analysis

In this exercise, we will create each of the following interactively, and then capture scripts that JMP will generate for us:

- Summary table from the original data
- Overlay Plot with connecting lines

Interactive Steps

Our first task will be to open a JMP data table containing data about a class of students. Next, we will summarize the data by creating a Summary table that produces the mean height for each age by gender.

1. From the **Help** menu, select **Sample Data**.

Figure 2.1 Sample Data Index

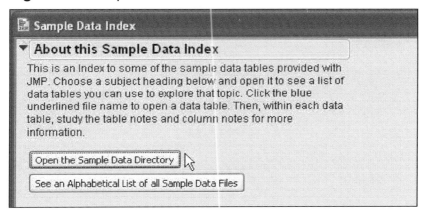

2. Click the **Open the Sample Data Directory** button.

3. Select the **Big Class.jmp** file, and then click **Open** to open the Big Class sample data table.

4. Close the **Sample Data Index**.

5. From the **Tables** menu, select **Summary**.

6. In the resulting dialog window:

   a. Select the **height** column.

   b. Click the **Statistics** button, and then select **Mean**.

   c. Select **age,** and then click the **Group** button.

   d. Select **sex,** and then click the **Subgroup** button.

   e. Click **OK**.

Figure 2.2 Summary Dialog Window

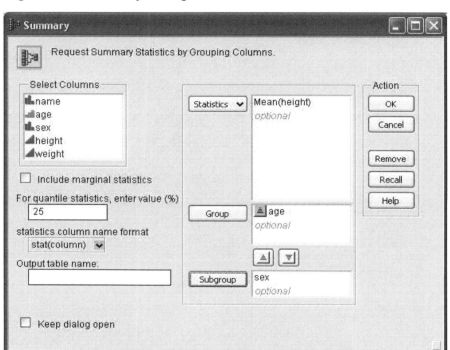

Next, we will create an Overlay Plot and connect the lines to identify any trends.

7. With the **Big Class By (age)** data table as the active table, select **Graph ▶ Overlay Plot** from the **Graph** menu.

8. In the resulting dialog window:

   a. Select the **Mean(height, F)** and **Mean(height, M)** columns.

   b. Click the **Y** button.

   c. Select **age**, and then click the **X** button.

   d. Click **OK**.

Figure 2.3 Overlay Plot Dialog Window

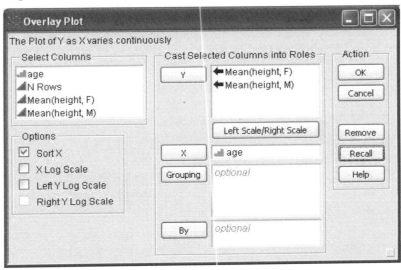

9. When the Overlay Plot appears, click the red triangle and select **Y Options** ▶
   Connect Points.

Figure 2.4 Connect Points

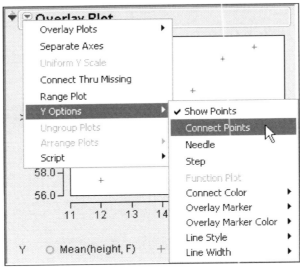

Now, we have created the Summary table and the Overlay Plot.

Figure 2.5 Summary Table and Overlay Plot

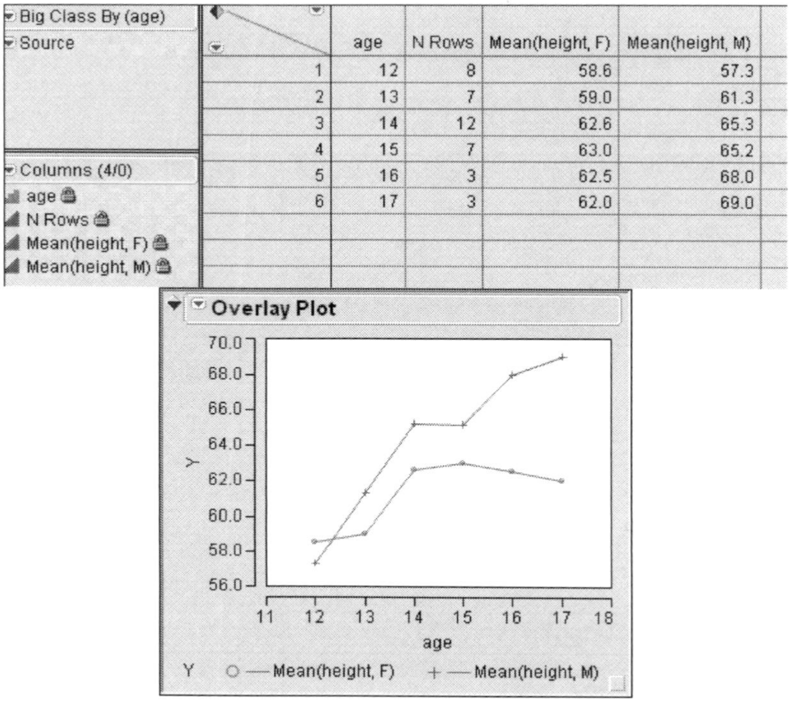

Next, we will extract the scripts that JMP generated for us and combine them in a single script.

Extracting the Scripts

Table scripts are a bit different in that you cannot simply save the script to a Script window like we could if we were saving the script from an analysis. Therefore, we will need to open a new Script window, where the scripts can be pasted.

1. From the **File** menu, select **New ▶ Script**.

2. From the **Window** menu, select **Big Class By (age)** to locate the Summary table.

3. When the Summary data table is in view, open the **Source** Table Script by clicking on the red triangle, and then select **Edit**.

Figure 2.6 Edit Summary Source Script

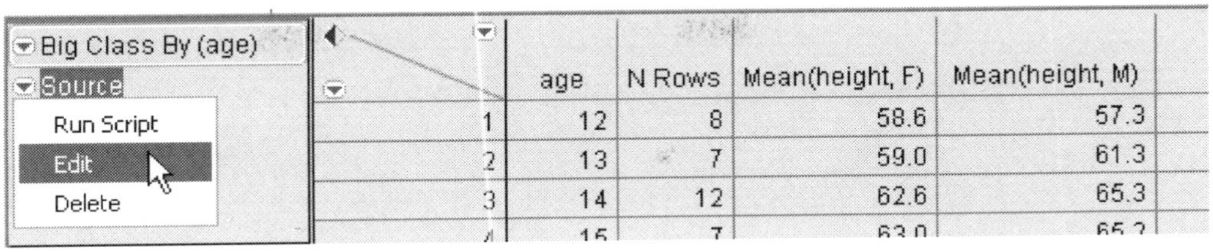

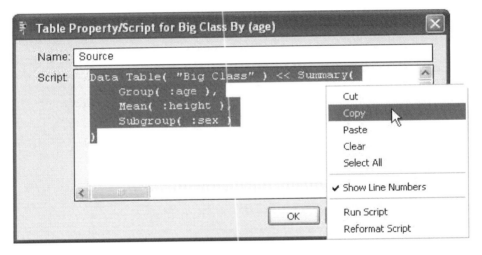

4. In the resulting window, select the entire script and copy it by right-clicking the script and selecting **Copy**.

Figure 2.7 View of Summary Source Script

5. Click **OK** to dismiss the Source Table Script window.

6. From the **Window** menu, select **Script** to locate your new Script window.

7. Paste the script by clicking on the **Edit** menu, and then select **Paste**.

8. Add a semicolon after the last closing parenthesis.

Figure 2.8 Pasted Summary Script

```
 Script
    1    Data Table( "Big Class" ) << Summary(
    2        Group( :age ),
    3        Mean( :height ),
    4        Subgroup( :sex )
    5    );
```

 Notice that the previous Script window displays line numbers. You can turn on the line numbers option by clicking the **File** menu and selecting **Preferences**. Scroll down to the **Script Editor** icon and check the box beside "Show line numbers."

Next, we will copy the Overlay Plot script.

1. From the **Window** menu, select **Big Class By (age)- Overlay Plot** to locate the Overlay Plot.

2. In the Overlay Plot window, click the red triangle, and then select **Script ▶ Copy Script**.

Figure 2.9 Copy Overlay Plot

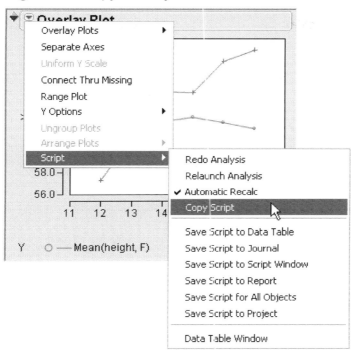

3. Go back to the Script window, and press the **Enter** key a couple of times to move the cursor down a few lines.

4. Paste the script into the Script window by selecting **Edit ▶ Paste**.

Figure 2.10 Paste Overlay Script

```
 Script
    1   Data Table( "Big Class" ) << Summary(
    2       Group( :age ),
    3       Mean( :height ),
    4       Subgroup( :sex )
    5   );
    6
    7   Overlay Plot(
    8       X( :age ),
    9       Y( :Name( "Mean(height, F)" ), :Name( "Mean(height, M)" ) ),
   10       Connect Points( 1 )
   11   )
```

5. Add a semicolon after the last closing parenthesis.

6. Use the **Window** menu to locate the **Big Class By (age)** data table, and then close it. Repeat these steps to locate and close **Big Class By (age)- Overlay Plot**.

Coding Changes

Now this script looks pretty good, but there is a problem.

If you run this code as it is, JMP might return error messages to the log as shown here.

```
/*:

Not Found in access or evaluation of 'Overlay Plot' ,
Bad Argument( {:Name( "Mean(height, F)" ), :Name(
"Mean(height, M)" )} )

, Overlay Plot(
    X( :age ),
    Y( :Name( "Mean(height, F)" ), :Name( "Mean(height,
M)" ) ),
    Connect Thru Missing( 1 )
)
```

(continued)

(continued)

```
In the following script, error marked by /*###*/
Data Table( "Big Class" ) << Summary(
    Group( :age ),
    Mean( :height ),
    Subgroup( :sex )
);
Overlay Plot(/*###*/X( :age ),
    Y( :Name( "Mean(height, F)" ), :Name( "Mean(height,
M)" ) ),
    Connect Thru Missing( 1 )
);
```

What does all that mean?

These error messages indicate that JMP cannot find the columns **Mean(height, F)** and **Mean(height, M)**. These columns are not found because JMP is looking at the original Big Class data table, rather than at the Summary table.

How do we correct this?

First, we assign a name (you can think of it as a nickname) to the Summary table using an assignment statement. This name is also known as a *global variable*. Global variables are references you assign that remain throughout the JMP session.

 Unlike other languages, it is not necessary to first declare the global variable. Simply assign it to an object, like a data table, and start using it!

1. In the script, set the Summary table name to be **sumDT** as shown in Figure 2.11.

Figure 2.11 Data Table Name Assignment

```
 Script
   1    sumDT = Data Table( "Big Class" ) << Summary(
   2        Group( :age ),
   3        Mean( :height ),
   4        Subgroup( :sex )
   5    );
   6
```

In this example, **sumDT** will continue to represent the **Big Class By (age)** Summary table until the data table is closed, **sumDT** gets redefined, or you close JMP.

Next, we will tell JMP that the Overlay Plot should be created using the data stored in the Summary table rather than in the original **Big Class** data table.

In order to accomplish this task, it is important to understand that JSL is a powerful object-oriented-*like* language that is built upon the concept of *sending* messages to JMP objects in order to tell them what to do.

Here is the basic form of a JSL statement:

```
object << Message( Argument );
```

where **<<** represents the send operator.

2. In the script, send the Overlay Plot message to the Summary data table by adding **sumDT** (as the object) and the send operator (**<<**), as shown in Figure 2.12.

Figure 2.12 Data Table Specified

```
Script
1   sumDT = Data Table( "Big Class" ) << Summary(
2       Group( :age ),
3       Mean( :height ),
4       Subgroup( :sex )
5   );
6
7   sumDT << Overlay Plot(
8       X( :age ),
9       Y( :Name( "Mean(height, F)" ), :Name( "Mean(height, M)" ) ),
10      Connect Thru Missing( 1 )
11  );
```

After making these changes, the code will run successfully.

3. From the **Edit** menu, select **Run Script**.

Figure 2.13 Sample 2 Results

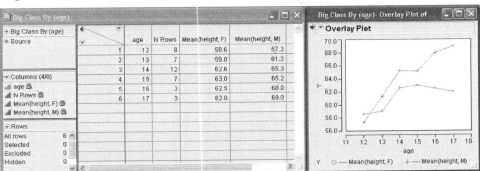

4. With the Script window active, click the **File** menu, and then select **Save As**.

5. Browse to the same location as the previous example, name the script **Sample2.JSL**, and then click **Save**.

Figure 2.14 Save Sample2.JSL

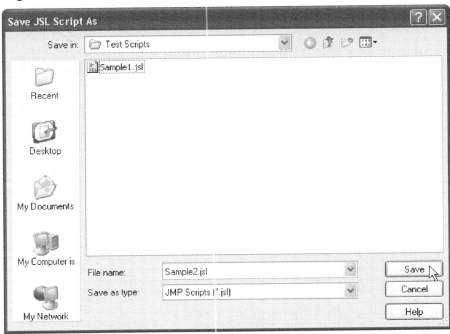

Stitching Together the Import of Text Data, a Summary Table, and Two Analyses

Now that you've seen how easy it is to combine scripts of various tasks into one script, we are going to show you something a little more interesting. In this sample, we put together a script that brings in elements from the scripts that you previously saved.

 If you are following along from the previous sample, close all open analyses, and close the Script window. To do this, click the **Window** menu, and then select **Close All**.

Extracting the Scripts

Because we are bringing in scripts that we stored in JSL files, there won't be any scripts to capture interactively from JMP. Instead, we will open Sample1.JSL and Sample2.JSL and extract the desired sections of code in order to build the new script.

To begin, open a new Script window by clicking on the **File** menu and select **New ▶ Script**. This is where we will build the main script.

Next, extract the code from the **Sample1.JSL** file:

1. From the **File** menu, select **Open**.

2. Ensure the **Files of type** field is set to *All JMP Files*.

3. Navigate to the location where you saved the **Sample1.JSL** file, and then select the file.

4. Click **Open**.

5. Select the entire script, and then copy it by right-clicking and selecting **Copy** from the menu.

6. Go back to your main Script window by selecting **Window ▶ Script.**

7. Paste the script by selecting **Edit ▶ Paste.**

Figure 2.15 Paste Sample1.JSL

```
 1   Open(
 2       "C:\Program Files\SAS\JMP\8\Support Files English\Sample Import Data\Bigclass_L.txt",
 3       columns(
 4           name = Character,
 5           age = Numeric,
 6           sex = Character,
 7           height = Numeric,
 8           weight = Numeric
 9       ),
10       Import Settings(
11           End Of Line( CRLF, CR, LF ),
12           End Of Field( Tab, Comma ),
13           Strip Quotes( 1 ),
14           Use Apostrophe as Quotation Mark( 0 ),
15           Scan Whole File( 1 ),
16           Labels( 1 ),
17           Column Names Start( 1 ),
18           Data Starts( 2 ),
19           Lines To Read( All ),
20           Year Rule( "10-90" )
21       )
22   );
23
24   Distribution( Continuous Distribution( Column( :age ) ) );
```

8. Locate and close the **Sample1** Script window by selecting **Window** ▶ **Sample1**. Then from the **File** menu, select **Close**.

So far in the script, we have instructed JMP to import a text file and create a Distribution analysis from it. Next, we will paste in the script from **Sample 2** at the end of our current script.

1. From the **File** menu, select **Open**.

2. Ensure the **Files of type** field is set to *All JMP Files*.

3. Navigate to the location where you saved the **Sample2.JSL** file, and then select the file.

4. Click **Open**.

5. Select the entire script, then copy by right-clicking and selecting **Copy** from the menu.

6. Go back to your main Script window by selecting **Window** ▶ **Script**.

7. Press the **Enter** key a couple of times to move the cursor down a few lines below the Distribution.

8. Paste the script by selecting **Edit** ▶ **Paste**.

Figure 2.16 Paste Sample2.JSL

```
25
26   sumDT = Data Table( "Big Class" ) << Summary(
27       Group( :age ),
28       Mean( :height ),
29       Subgroup( :sex )
30   );
31
32   sumDT << Overlay Plot(
33       X( :age ),
34       Y( :Name( "Mean(height, F)" ), :Name( "Mean(height, M)" ) ),
35       Connect Thru Missing( 1 )
36   );
```

9. Locate and close the **Sample2** Script window by selecting **Sample2** from the **Window** menu. Then from the **File** menu, select **Close**.

Coding Changes

Now, once again we have created a script that looks good but will not run successfully.

Why, not? The messages in the log provide a significant hint as shown here:

```
Data Table not found open. Do you want to open a file?

Cannot locate data table in access or evaluation of
'Data Table' , Data Table( "Big Class" )
```

And further down you will see the location of the error by the **/*####*/** marks.

```
sumDT = Data Table/*####*/("Big Class") << Summary(
    Group( :age ),
    Mean( :height ),
    Subgroup( :sex )
);
```

 If your Log window is closed, you can view it by selecting **Log** from the **View** menu.

The problem in this example is that the data table we want our Summary table created from is not named **Big Class** but rather, **Bigclass_L**. There are a couple of ways to correct this problem.

- Hard-code the table name by specifying it in the Data Table argument.

```
sumDT = Data Table( "Bigclass_L" ) << Summary(
    Group( :age ),
    Mean( :height ),
    Subgroup( :sex )
);
```

- Assign a global variable to the data table when it is imported, and use the global variable name in place of the Data Table command. This option might require slightly more coding, but actually allows for greater flexibility. See Figure 2.17.

Figure 2.17 Final Script

```
1  dt = Open(
2      "C:\Program Files\SAS\JMP\8\Support Files English\Sample Import Data\Bigclass_L.txt",
3      columns(
4          name = Character,
5          age = Numeric,
6          sex = Character,
7          height = Numeric,
8          weight = Numeric
9      ),
10     Import Settings(
11         End Of Line( CRLF, CR, LF ),
12         End Of Field( Tab, Comma ),
13         Strip Quotes( 1 ),
14         Use Apostrophe as Quotation Mark( 0 ),
15         Scan Whole File( 1 ),
16         Labels( 1 ),
17         Column Names Start( 1 ),
18         Data Starts( 2 ),
19         Lines To Read( All ),
20         Year Rule( "10-90" )
21     )
22 );
23
24 Distribution( Continuous Distribution( Column( :age ) ) );
25
26 sumDT = dt << Summary(
27     Group( :age ),
28     Mean( :height ),
29     Subgroup( :sex )
30 );
31
32 sumDT << Overlay Plot(
33     X( :age ),
34     Y( :Name( "Mean(height, F)" ), :Name( "Mean(height, M)" ) ),
35     Connect Thru Missing( 1 )
36 )
```

After making the changes noted in Figure 2.17, run your script to see the results.

Figure 2.18 Sample 3 Results

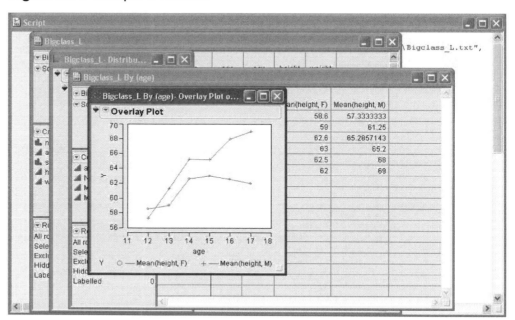

Now that you have a script that does everything your manager wants, save the script to your desired location, and name it **WeeklyReport.jsl**.

You are finished! You have put together an entire script that will:

- Import text data
- Create a Distribution of the data
- Summarize the data
- Create an Overlay Plot from the summarized data

And, all of this has been done with very little code written by you.

Creating a Custom Toolbar Button That Will Execute a Script (Windows and Linux Only)

You could keep your WeeklyReport script as a JSL file because JSL files are a great place to store scripts so they can be opened and executed in the future.

Or perhaps, you would rather click a button and have JMP perform all those tasks for you at once.

In this section, we will demonstrate how you can save your script as a custom toolbar button. In fact, you could share the toolbar button with your manager so that he will be able to run his own reports.

First, you will need to create a location for your toolbar button.

1. From the **Edit** menu, select **Customize** ▶ **Menus and Toolbars**.

2. Expand the **Toolbars** item and the **Graph** item.

3. Right-click the item above or below where you want to place the new toolbar item.

4. Select **Insert Before** or **Insert After** from the menu, as appropriate.

Figure 2.19 Insert Before

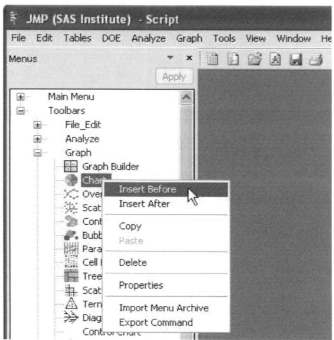

JMP will give the new item you created the name **Untitled**. You now have a location for your script.

5. To finish setting up the new toolbar item, right-click **Untitled**, and then select **Properties** from the context menu.

Figure 2.20 Button Properties

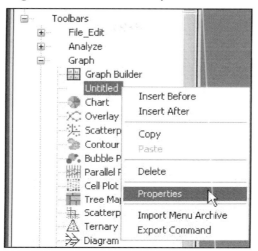

The Toolbar Button Properties dialog window provides the interface where you set up your custom toolbar button. Note the three tabs: **General**, **Icon**, and **Shortcut**.

Figure 2.21 Toolbar Button Properties Dialog Window

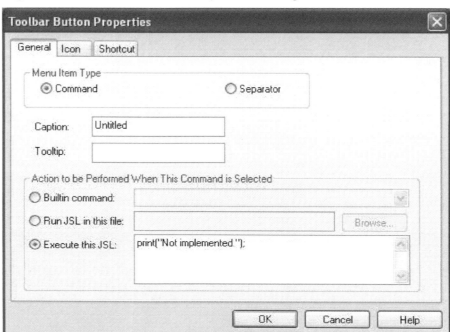

6. Click the **General** tab to construct the basic properties for your button.

7. Set the **Menu Item Type** by clicking the **Command** button.

8. Enter a unique name in the **Caption** field.

9. Though not required, **Tooltip** is an option for conveying information when the cursor is placed over your custom button. Enter a description in the **Tooltip** field.

Then there's the important part regarding your JSL code, because there are three options:

- The **Builtin Command** is for cases where you may want to use one of JMP's existing platform scripts.

- If you select **Run JSL in this file**, you must point JMP to where your JSL file is stored. This option is a good choice for large scripts or scripts you may want to open and change frequently.

- The last option is **Execute this JSL**. When using this option, you would paste the code directly into the dialog. This is the preferred option for small scripts.

Figure 2.22 General Tab Completed

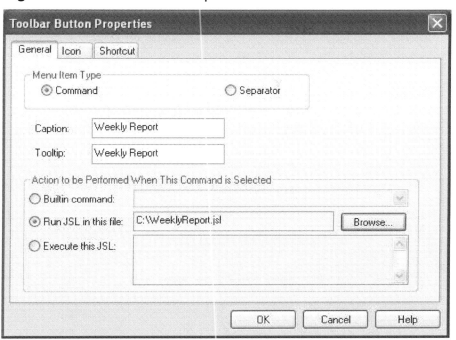

10. Choose **Run JSL in this file** and point JMP to the location where WeeklyReport.JSL is stored.

11. Click the **Icon** tab to set up an icon for your custom button.

JMP offers a list of icons available for selection in the drop-down list for **Builtin Icon ID**, or you can provide a link to a bitmap image file through the **Use Bitmap** option.

12. Select the **IDB_EDIT_SUBMIT_SCRIPT** item in the menu.

Figure 2.23 Menu of Icons That Are Provided by JMP

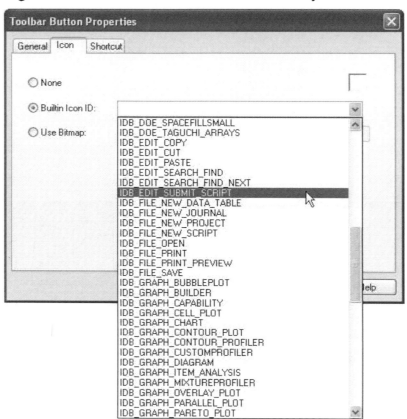

Another JMP option is a keyboard shortcut for your button. To create a shortcut, click the **Shortcut** tab. The important thing to remember here is to pick a shortcut that is NOT already being used by JMP. Fortunately, JMP provides a list of the current accelerators/keyboard shortcuts.

13. Add a keyboard shortcut by placing a **Z** in the **Accelerator Key** field, and then select the **Ctrl** and **Shift** checkboxes.

Figure 2.24 Keyboard Shortcuts

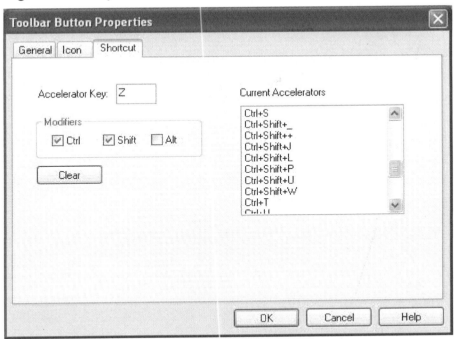

14. When you're finished with the setup, click the **OK** button and review the results in the Toolbars list.

15. To apply your addition, click the **Apply** button, and you will see your new button.

 If you are following along with these steps, you will need to ensure the Graph Toolbar is visible. To display the Graph Toolbar, click the **View** menu, and then select **Show Toolbars**. Select the **Graph** checkbox, and then click **OK**.

Figure 2.25 Toolbar Menu and Graph Toolbar with Added Button

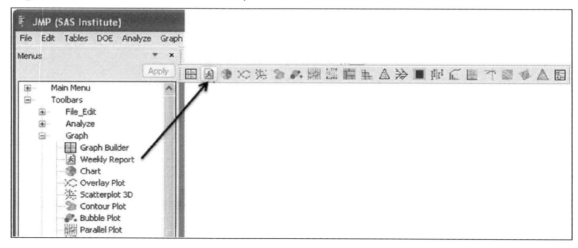

16   Click the **X** located above the **Apply** button to close the Menu and Toolbars list.

17. When prompted to save your changes, click **Yes**.

 To clear any menu or toolbar customizations, select **Edit ▶ Customize ▶ Revert to Factory Defaults**. You will be prompted to verify your intentions, and then you will be notified where you can access a backup of the previous settings.

Would you rather have a custom menu item than a toolbar button? To create a menu item for your script, follow the same directions for creating the toolbar button, but expand the **Main Menu** tree to create a location for your new menu item.

Summary

These are the basics that should get you scripting very quickly. Following are the key things to keep in mind:

- Perform your analysis interactively first.
- Extract scripts from JMP as the foundation for your script.
- Stitch the scripts together by assigning names to objects, such as data tables.
- Don't forget to add semicolons between statements.

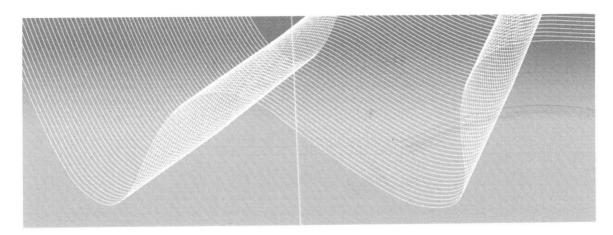

Chapter Three

The Double-Layer Cake

Overview

You now have the script to import your data and create your report. Once again, your manager says he wants you to add a few refinements, maybe add a few items, and delete some others. In order to manipulate the elements of a report, you need to understand how it is constructed. In this chapter, you will learn about:

- Folding back the layers of the results
- The analysis layer
- The report layer
  - □ Presentation options
  - □ Display boxes
  - □ Accessing items in a report
  - □ Adding items in a report
  - □ Deleting items from a report
  - □ Saving report tables

Folding Back the Layers of the Results

JMP creates a platform object when you launch any platform from the **Analyze** or **Graph** menus. When developing scripts, it is important to understand how the platform object is constructed in order to customize it using JSL. Think of the platform object consisting of two layers, similar to a double layer cake:

- The analysis layer provides access to all the options available through the red triangle menus.
- The report layer provides access to all the options available through context menus, in other words, those options that are available when you right-click within the platform results.

Figure 3.1 Cake and the JMP Report

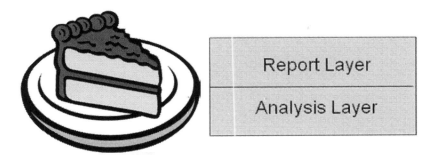

The Analysis Layer

Let's take a look at each level, starting with the analysis layer. The options for the analysis layer can be viewed in the red triangle icon drop-down menu of the report. For example, after you launch the Distribution platform and create a report, click on the red triangle icon to the left of the response variable, and you will see a menu with a number of options that can be turned on and off, as designated by the presence or absence of checkmarks.

Figure 3.2 Menu That Shows the Platform Options for Distributions

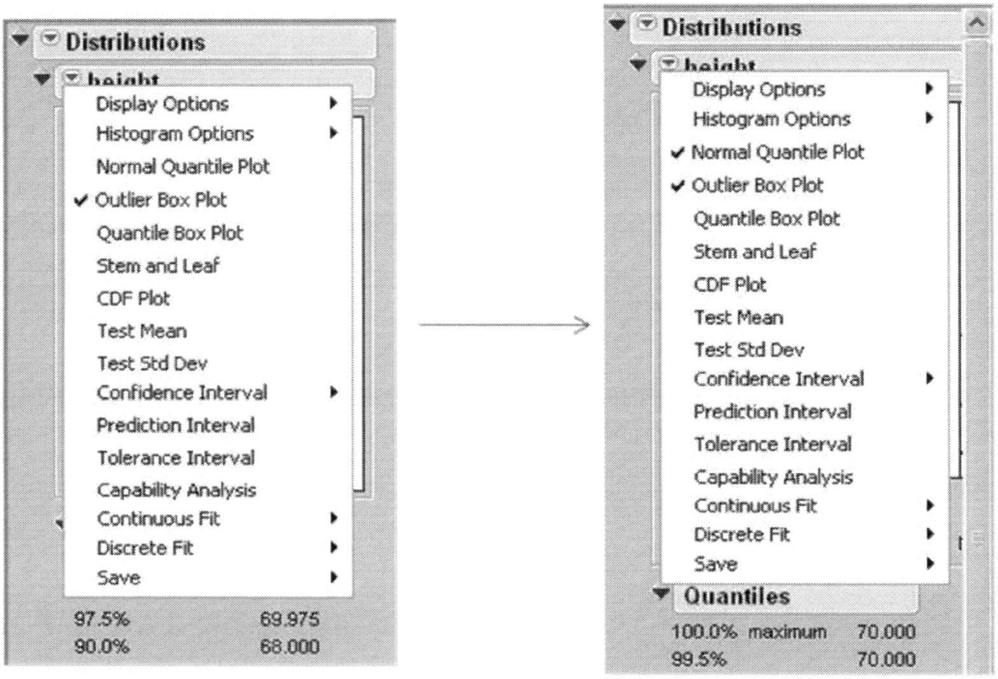

As you know, when selecting an option that was not previously selected, more information is added to the report. In this example, a Normal Quantile plot was requested.

Figure 3.3 The Normal Quantile Plot Is Added

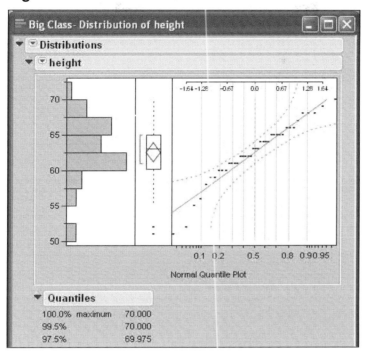

The same options you select or deselect interactively in the red triangle icon menu can also be applied in JSL.

There are two methods for including platform options in JSL.

- You can specify the options *in* the platform launch:

  ```
  dist = Distribution( Y( height ), Normal Quantile Plot( 1 ),
  Outlier Box Plot( 0 ) );
  ```

- Or, you can send messages to the platform object *after* the launch:

  ```
  dist << Normal Quantile Plot( 1 );

  dist << Outlier Box Plot( 0 );
  ```

The options can be turned on by using '1' as the argument, and turned off by using '0' as the argument. In JSL, using '1' in an argument indicates 'True' and turns an option on, and using '0' in an argument means 'False' and turns an option off.

Figure 3.4 Two Methods That Perform the Same Task

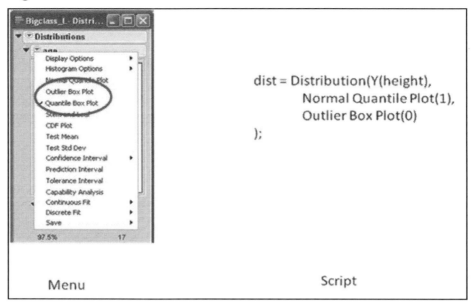

Besides looking at the drop-down menus, how can you find out all the options available for a platform object? One method is to execute a **Show Properties** command and view the log for the details:

```
dist = Distribution( Y( height ) );

Show Properties( dist );
```

Figure 3.5 The Log Window

```
Log
Uniform Scaling [Boolean]
Stack [Boolean]
Vertical [Boolean] [Scripting Only]
Script [Subtable]
   Redo Analysis [Action](Rerun this same analysis in a new window. The analysis will be different if the data has
   Relaunch Analysis [Action](Return to the launcher for this analysis.)
   Automatic Recalc [Boolean](Redo the analysis automatically for exclude and data changes.)
   Copy Script [Action](Create a script (JSL) to produce this analysis, and put it on the clipboard.)
   Save Script to Data Table [Action](Create a script (JSL) to produce this analysis, and save it as a table proper
   Save Script to Journal [Action](Create a script (JSL) to produce this analysis, and add a Button to the journal
   Save Script to Script Window [Action](Create a script (JSL) to produce this analysis, and append it to the curre
   Save Script to Report [Action](Create a script (JSL) to produce this analysis, and show it in the report itself.
   Save Script for All Objects [Action](Look at the all the live scriptable objects owned by reports in this window
   Save Script to Project [Action](Create a script (JSL) to produce this analysis, and save it in a project.)
   Get Script [Action] [Scripting Only]
   Get Script With Datatable [Action] [Scripting Only]
   Get Data Table [Action] [Scripting Only]
```

Figure 3.5 shows the Log window that results after you perform the **Show Properties** command on the **Distribution** reference.

The second method is to view a dedicated index, the *Object Scripting Index*, in the JMP Help. Select **Help** ▶ **Indexes** ▶ **Object Scripting**, and select the platform object from the list (see Figure 3.6).

Figure 3.6 Highlighting of Distribution in the Object Scripting Index

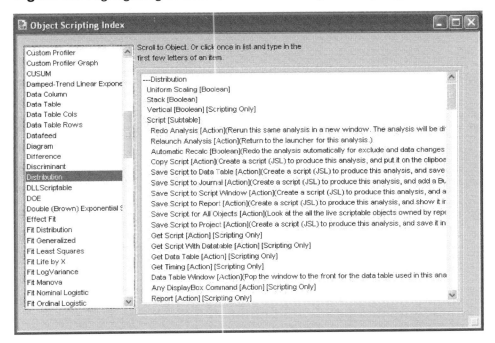

As Figure 3.6 shows, when you highlight **Distribution** in the *Object Scripting Index*, the messages that are available for that platform object are displayed.

Note that some options are followed by the designation: **[Scripting Only]**. This designation means the option is available only through scripting, and you cannot access it through the interactive interface. Therefore, it is to your advantage to review the details for an object either through **Show Properties** or through the **Object Index**; otherwise, you might miss something that could be useful for your scripting project.

The Report Layer

The report layer is made up of presentation options and display boxes. Let's look at each of these items in detail.

Presentation Options

Interactively, you can make changes to the report layer by right-clicking and selecting options from the context menu; for example, you can add a legend or change the background color.

Figure 3.7 Context Menu Launched from a Bivariate Plot

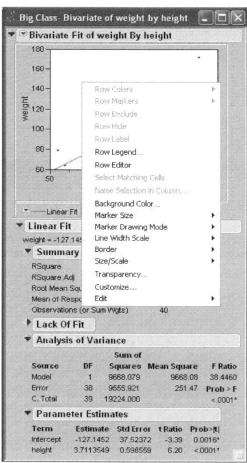

How do you access these same options using JSL?

Earlier in this chapter, you used the platform object when accessing the analysis layer. To do the same for the report layer, you need to send the **Report** command to the platform object. Let's look at two methods for performing this task.

- In the following code, a reference is first created for the Bivariate results that we arbitrarily named **biv**. We send the report message to the Bivariate reference and name it **repBiv**:

```
biv = Bivariate( Y( :weight ), X( :height ) );

repBiv = biv << Report;
```

- You can also wrap the message around the analysis layer reference:

```
biv = Bivariate( Y( :weight ), X( :height ) );

repBiv = Report( biv );
```

Now we have the first step in accessing the report layer. However, before we can send messages with the report reference, we must understand how the report is organized and constructed.

Display Boxes

The basic building blocks of any JMP report are the display boxes. There are many types of display boxes, and each has its own set of messages. How do you know which display boxes are used in a report? And, if there is more than one of that type of display box, how do you know which one to reference? You might not be able to determine this by looking at the report. JMP actually has a built-in feature that shows the arrangement of the display boxes. To view this feature, right-click a blue-inverted triangle icon in a report. From the drop-down menu, select **Edit ▶ Show Tree Structure**.

 For releases prior to JMP 8, press and hold the **CTRL + SHIFT** keys while you right-click a blue-inverted triangle icon in a report.

Figure 3.8 Tree Structure of a Bivariate Report

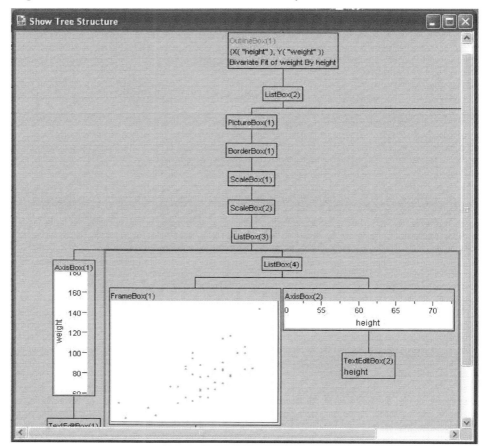

JMP draws a diagram showing the different display boxes in the report. Note the OutlineBox, AxisBox, FrameBox, and PictureBox in Figure 3.8. These are basic constructors found in most reports, and there is a number associated with each constructor. Knowing the type and number of the display box will allow you to reference individual display boxes in a JMP report. Let's explore using some of the common types of display boxes.

FrameBox

Suppose you want to enlarge your Bivariate plot. To change the size of the graph interactively, you could right-click the plot and select **Size/Scale** ▶ **Frame Size** in the context menu (see Figure 3.9).

Figure 3.9 Accessing the Frame Size Interactively

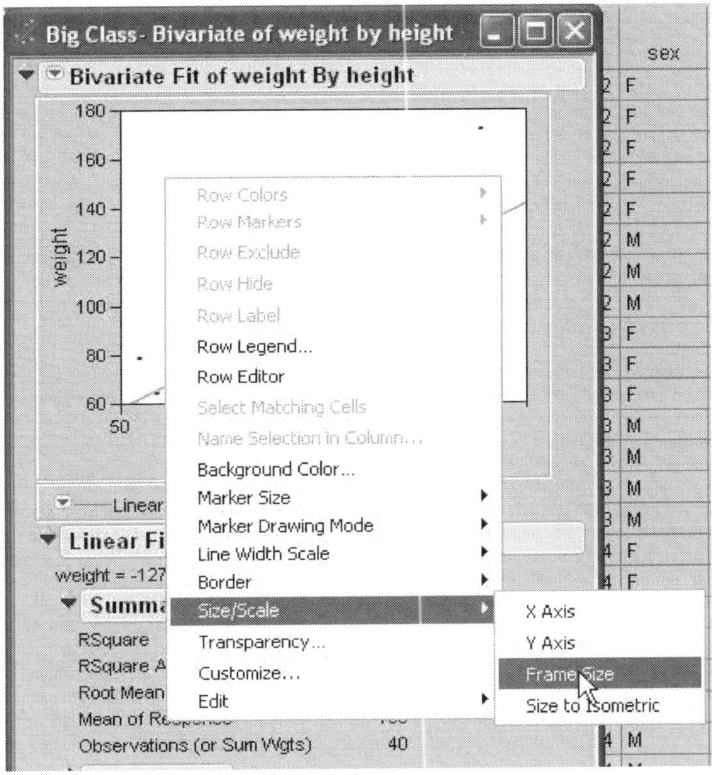

A window appears where you can specify the horizontal and vertical size of the plot in pixels.

Figure 3.10 The Frame Size Window

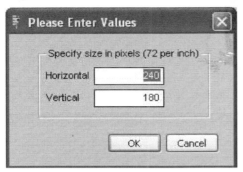

To perform this same action in JSL, first determine what type of display box you need to reference. In the display tree, the display box that holds the plot is the FrameBox, and it is the first FrameBox created in the report; therefore, it is designated FrameBox(1).

Figure 3.11 Display Tree of the Bivariate Report

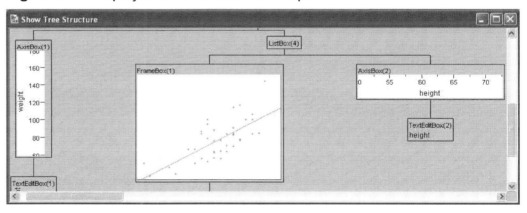

To determine what message to send to this FrameBox, go to the DisplayBox Scripting Index by selecting **Help ▶ Indexes ▶ DisplayBox Scripting**. Browse to **FrameBox** and highlight it.

Figure 3.12 Messages for FrameBox

Note that many of the options have the same names as can be found on the interactive menu. In the list of available messages for FrameBox, there is one for **Frame Size**, under the **Size/Scale** topic. Following are the scripting statements needed to create the plot and change the frame size of the Bivariate plot:

```
biv = Bivariate( Y( :weight ), X( :height ), Fit Line );

repBiv = biv << Report;

repBiv[FrameBox( 1 )] << Frame Size( 250, 400 );
```

Figure 3.13 The Results of Executing the Script

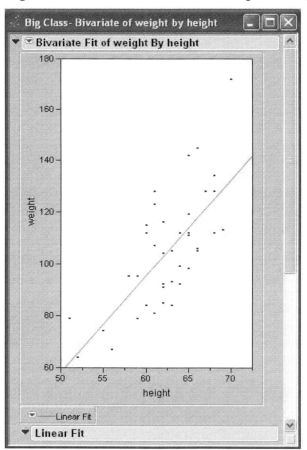

AxisBox

Perhaps you want to change the scale of the X axis of a graph. Interactively, you can right-mouse click the axis and select **Axis Settings**.

Figure 3.14 Accessing Axis Settings Interactively

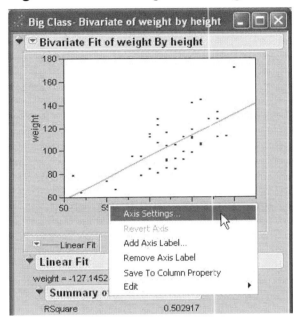

A window appears where you can change the **Minimum**, **Maximum**, and **Increment** of the X axis scale (see Figure 3.15).

Figure 3.15 X Axis Specification Dialog Window

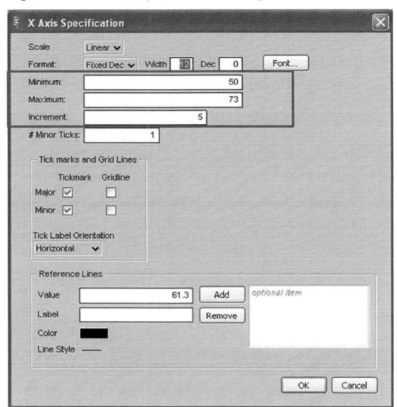

To send a message to an AxisBox, determine which AxisBox represents the X axis by looking again at the Display Tree Structure for this report. The X axis is represented by AxisBox(2).

Figure 3.16 X Axis Is AxisBox(2)

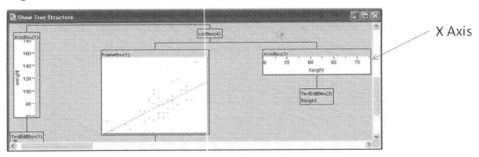

Go back to the DisplayBox Scripting Index and locate **AxisBox**.

Figure 3.17 AxisBox Messages

Look at the messages for AxisBox. Under **Scale** are the messages for **Min**, **Max**, and **Inc**. There are two ways to send these messages to the AxisBox. One way is to send the message as a combined `Axis Settings()` command:

```
repBiv[Axisbox( 2 )] << Axis Settings( Min( 45 ), Max( 70 ),
Inc( 10 ) );
```

The other way is to send the message as individual commands:

```
repBiv[Axisbox( 2 )] << Min( 45 );
repBiv[Axisbox( 2 )] << Max( 70 );
repBiv[Axisbox( 2 )] << Inc( 10 );
```

OutlineBox

Let's talk about a basic structure that is part of all JMP platform-generated reports: the OutlineBox. The OutlineBox represents a node, which is a single component of a JMP report. The typical JMP report has several of these nodes, which are arranged vertically to form a hierarchy.

Figure 3.18 OutlineBox Hierarchy In a Oneway Report

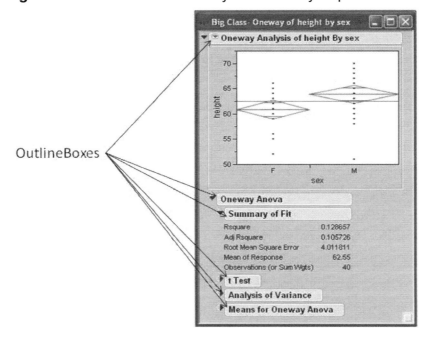

Note that in Figure 3.18, the contents of the **Summary of Fit** node are visible, while those of **t Test**, **Analysis of Variance**, and **Means for Oneway Anova** are not. To open those last three nodes interactively, you can click the blue disclosure icon on the left of each outline node. Clicking the blue disclosure triangle icon toggles a node open or closed.

To perform the same action using JSL, you need to send a message to the OutlineBox of interest. For example, in Figure 3.19, when the report is created, all OutlineBoxes are open.

```
ow = Oneway(
    Y( :height ),
    X( :sex ),
    Means( 1 ),
    Box Plots( 0 ),
    Mean Diamonds( 1 )
);
```

Figure 3.19 Oneway with Open OutlineBox Nodes

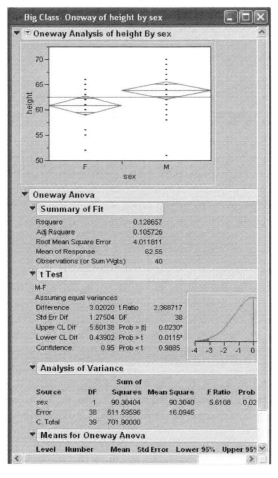

To close the t Test node, send a message to the OutlineBox. In addition to the report message to the Oneway reference, refer to the specific OutlineBox by its text string:

```
Report( ow )["t Test"]
```

What message to the OutlineBox will close the node? Check the DisplayBox Scripting Index by selecting **Help ▶ Indexes ▶ DisplayBox Scripting**, and then select **OutlineBox**. The first entry under the topic is **Close[Boolean]**. In scripting, the word Boolean means using '1' in an argument to indicate 'true' and using '0'in an argument to indicate 'false'. In this case, to close the node use '1':

```
Report( ow )["t Test"] << Close( 1 );
```

Figure 3.20 Oneway Report with Closed OutlineBox Node

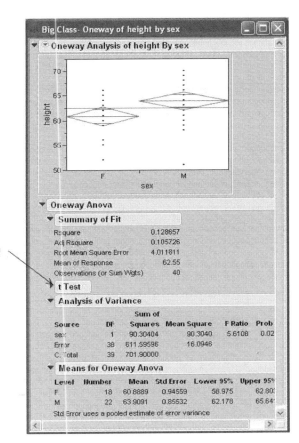

Closed outlineBox node

Accessing Items in a Report

How do you get a value out of a report and place it in a variable so that you can use it in another part of your script? We will show you an example where you extract the R square value from a Oneway report.

Following is the JSL code that is used to generate the report:

```
dt = Open( "$SAMPLE_DATA/Big Class.jmp" );
ow = dt << Oneway( Y( :height ), X( :sex ),
                   Means( 1 ), Mean Diamonds( 1 ) );
```

Figure 3.21 Oneway Report

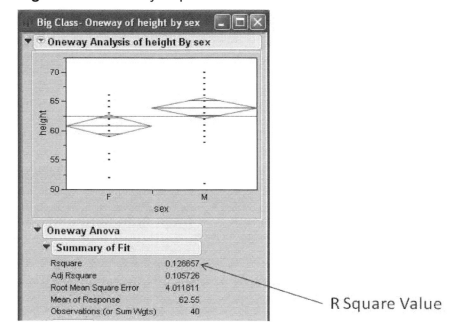

The R square value appears under the Summary of Fit area of the report.

Now to drill down to the value, you need to know more about the construction of the information in the Summary of Fit area. The best way to get started is to look at the tree structure. This time, right-click the blue triangle next to Summary of Fit and select **Edit**
▶ **Show Tree Structure**.

Figure 3.22 Tree Structure for Summary of Fit Area

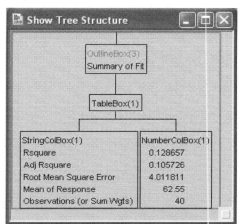

In the tree structure in Figure 3.22, locate the TableBox. The TableBox is the container for the Summary of Fit table. Here it comprises a StringColBox and a NumberColBox. The value that we want to access is the first value in the NumberColBox. Use subscripts to drill down to that value as follows:

```
myRsquare = Report( ow )[Number Col Box( 1 )][1];

Show( myRsquare );
```

Following is the output in the Log window:

```
/*:

myRsquare:0.12865656133928
```

You have successfully extracted the Rsquare value from the Summary of Fit table.

Adding Items to a Report

Suppose you want to add a few notes to the report. For example, to add a note at the bottom of an OutlineBox node, use the **Append** message:

```
ow = Oneway( Y( :height ), X( :sex ), Means( 1 ), Mean
Diamonds( 1 ) );

Report( ow )["Summary of Fit"] << Append( Text Box( "Note the
number of observations" ) );
```

Figure 3.23 Text Appended to an OutlineBox

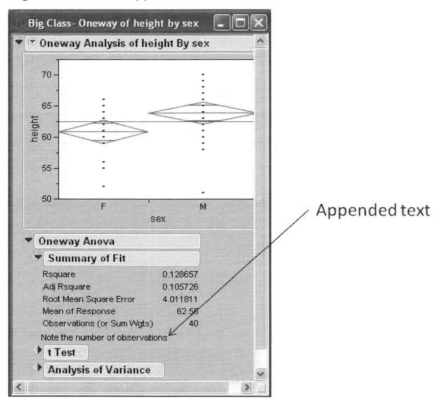

Appended text

To place the text at the top of the node, use the **Prepend** message as follows:

```
Report( ow )["Summary of Fit"] << Prepend( Text Box( "Note the
number of observations" ) );
```

Figure 3.24 Text Added to the Top of an OutlineBox

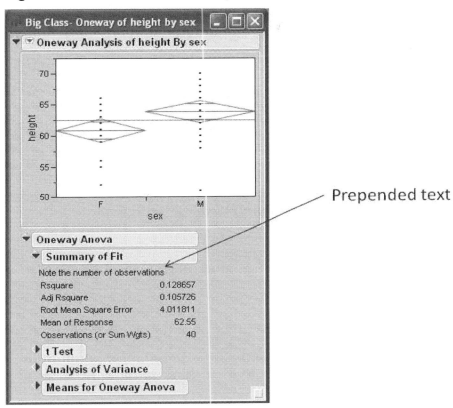

Prepended text

Deleting Items from a Report

It is also possible to delete items from a report. You can delete an entire Outline Box and its contents:

```
Report( ow )["Summary of Fit"] << Delete;
```

Figure 3.25 Summary of Fit Node Is Deleted from Oneway Report

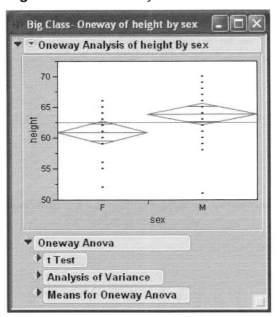

Saving Report Tables

JMP gives you the convenience of saving report tables as data tables interactively by right-clicking a section of the report, and then selecting **Make into data table**.

Figure 3.26 Context Menu Selection for Making a Data Table

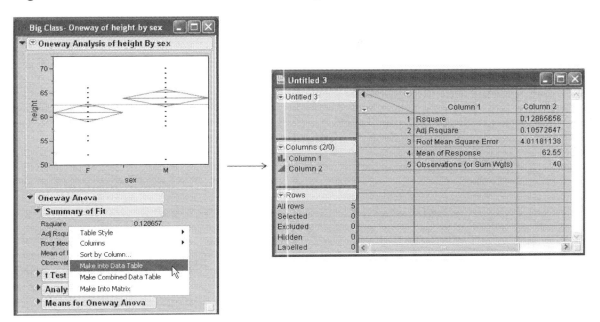

This action can be done in JSL, too:

```
ow = Oneway( Y( :height ), X( :sex ), Means( 1 ), Mean
Diamonds( 1 ) );

Report( ow )[Table Box( 1 )] << Make Into Data Table;
```

Here a reference was made to the TableBox. The TableBox is the container for the table, as seen in the tree structure, and it typically includes StringColBoxes and/or NumberColBoxes. When sending the `Make Into Data Table` message to the TableBox, the contents of both StringColBoxes and NumberColBoxes are included in the new table.

Figure 3.27 Tree Structure Diagram for the Summary of Fit Node

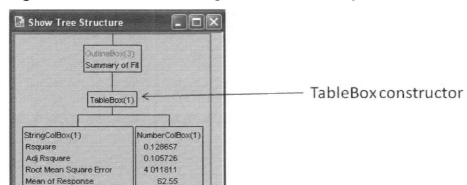

When using a By variable, a report object for each By member is packaged in the same report window:

```
ow = Oneway( Y( :height ), X( :sex ),
        Means( 1 ), Mean Diamonds( 1 ), by( :age ) );
```

Figure 3.28 By Variable Report

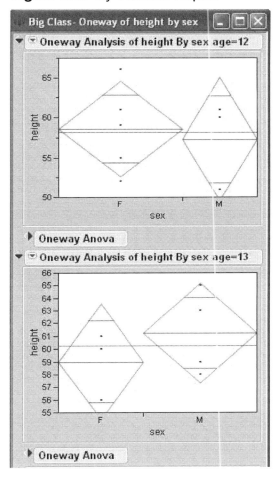

You can see how this works by using the **Show** command on the Oneway reference:

```
Show( ow );
```

```
/*:

ow:{Oneway[], Oneway[], Oneway[],
     Oneway[], Oneway[], Oneway[]}
```

JMP provides a convenient method for making one table for all the related member
nodes. For example, interactively, you would right-click one of the Summary of Fit
TableBoxes, and then select **Make Combined Data Table** to create one table for all the
Summary of Fit data in the report. This can be done in JSL, also. Because ow represents a
list of Oneway analyses, we must use a subscript to identify which Oneway analysis we
want to access. Note that the first Oneway object is referenced as ow[1]:

```
ow = Oneway( Y( :height ), X( :sex ), Means( 1 ),
             Mean Diamonds( 1 ), by( :age ) );

Report( ow [1])[Table Box( 1 )]
        << Make Combined Data Table;
```

Figure 3.29 Table with Combined Summary of Fit Data from All By Members of the Report

	age	X	Y	Column 1	Column 2
1	12	sex	height	Rsquare	0.01663211
2	12	sex	height	Adj Rsquare	-0.1472625
3	12	sex	height	Root Mean Square Error	5.4446712
4	12	sex	height	Mean of Response	58.125
5	12	sex	height	Observations (or Sum Wgts)	8
6	13	sex	height	Rsquare	0.15657216
7	13	sex	height	Adj Rsquare	-0.0121134
8	13	sex	height	Root Mean Square Error	3.05777697
9	13	sex	height	Mean of Response	60.2857143
10	13	sex	height	Observations (or Sum Wgts)	7
11	14	sex	height	Rsquare	0.3411583
12	14	sex	height	Adj Rsquare	0.27527413
13	14	sex	height	Root Mean Square Error	2.01565303
14	14	sex	height	Mean of Response	64.1666667
15	14	sex	height	Observations (or Sum Wgts)	12
16	15	sex	height	Rsquare	0.29156627
17	15	sex	height	Adj Rsquare	0.14987952
18	15	sex	height	Root Mean Square Error	1.83303028
19	15	sex	height	Mean of Response	64.5714286
20	15	sex	height	Observations (or Sum Wgts)	7
21	16	sex	height	Rsquare	0.61734694
22	16	sex	height	Adj Rsquare	0.23469388
23	16	sex	height	Root Mean Square Error	3.53553391
24	16	sex	height	Mean of Response	64.3333333
25	16	sex	height	Observations (or Sum Wgts)	3
26	17	sex	height	Rsquare	0.94230769
27	17	sex	height	Adj Rsquare	0.88461538
28	17	sex	height	Root Mean Square Error	1.41421356
29	17	sex	height	Mean of Response	66.6666667
30	17	sex	height	Observations (or Sum Wgts)	3

Summary

Now you have learned the basics of the JMP report and how the data and the display boxes for the data form the report. More importantly, you have observed how to modify the elements through scripting.

What's next? You will learn about resources and tips to make your scripting easier.

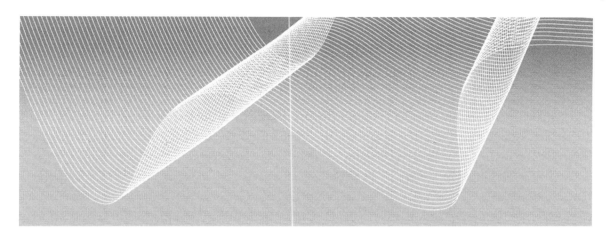

Chapter Four

Close Your Eyes and Jump!

Overview

You are almost ready to begin your journey of scripting on your own. You have learned how to give your scripting project a kick-start by letting JMP generate the initial script for you. You have learned how to put together various scripts that are generated by JMP. And you have learned how to access the layers of an analysis report.

So what's left?

In this chapter, you will learn about:

- Useful features of the Script Editor
- Resources available at your fingertips
- What to do in times of trouble
  - Common issues
  - Debugging tips

The Script Editor

As mentioned in Chapter One, the Script window is the workhorse of scripting. This window is also known as the *Script Editor* or *JSL Editor* and it is where you will primarily develop your scripting projects.

Essentially, the Script Editor is a simple text editor—but with some really cool features.

In this chapter, we will go over a few handy features, but a complete list of features can be found in the *JMP Scripting Guide*.

 You can develop your script code in any text editor. But once you learn all the features of the JMP Script Editor, we doubt you will want to use anything else!

There are several ways to access the Script Editor:

- From the **File** menu, select **New ▶ Script**.

- Click the **New Script** button on the JMP Starter.

- Click the **New Script** button on the toolbar.

- Press the **CTRL+T** keys.

Useful Features of the Script Editor

So what's so special about the Script Editor? Beginning with JMP 7, the Script Editor became much more user-friendly and helpful, too. Some of its cool features include:

- Highlighting of matching fences

- Automatic formatting

- Color coding

- Line numbers

Matching Fences

Because each opening parenthesis, curly brace, or square bracket needs a closing parenthesis, curly brace, or square bracket, the Script Editor offers highlighting so that you can quickly find their matches. This feature is very helpful when debugging your code.

Figure 4.1 Matching Parentheses

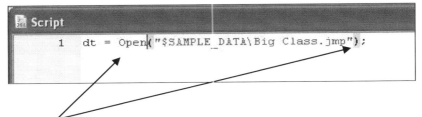

Notice the blue color for the opening and matched closing parentheses.

Also, when you type an opening parenthesis, curly brace, or square bracket, the Script Editor will automatically enter the closing parenthesis, curly brace, or square bracket for you.

If this feature is an annoyance, it can easily be disabled in the Script Editor Preferences. To access this setting, select **Preferences** from the **File** menu. Scroll down and click the **Script Editor** icon. Finally, uncheck the **Auto-complete Parentheses and Braces** option.

Automatic Formatting

The Script Editor's automatic formatting makes the script more readable because it uses consistent spacing and indentions throughout the script.

You can instruct JMP to format your script for you by simply right-clicking anywhere in the Script Editor window and selecting **Reformat Script**.

Figure 4.2 Before Reformatting Script

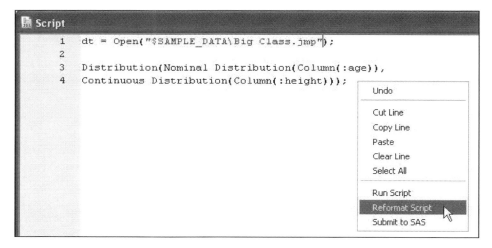

The reformatted script is shown in Figure 4.3.

Figure 4.3 After Reformatting Script

```
Script
1    dt = Open( "$SAMPLE_DATA\Big Class.jmp" );
2
3    Distribution(
4        Nominal Distribution( Column( :age ) ),
5        Continuous Distribution( Column( :weight ) )
6    );
```

Color Coding

Color coding makes it easy to recognize comments (green), strings (dark magenta), numerics (dark cyan and bold), and JSL commands (blue). These colors are the defaults and can be changed in the **Script Editor Preferences,** beginning in JMP 8.

Line Numbers

There are some options for customizing the Script Editor. In JMP Preferences (**File** ▶ **Preferences**), scroll down to the **Script Editor** icon:

Script Editor

Clicking this icon displays the options available for customizing the behavior of the Script Editor. Because all of these options are described in the *JMP Scripting Guide*, we won't go over each of them here. However, as mentioned briefly in Chapter Two, we will recommend that you turn on the **Show line numbers** option.

Having the line numbers present is very helpful when debugging your script, because the line number where the error was encountered is often included in the messages printed in the log.

Resources Available at Your Fingertips

As you begin your scripting projects, you might hit a roadblock or two. You know what you want JMP to do, but where do you go to find available message names or correct syntax if JMP didn't generate it for you?

There are several resources available to you that are filled with helpful information if you know how to access them:

- **Indexes:** From within JMP, select **Indexes** from the **Help** menu. As discussed in previous chapters, there are three indexes to help you find available functions and lists of messages that are appropriate for the object you are working with.

  □ The *JSL Functions* index contains a list of JSL commands and functions with the proper syntax, including arguments. This is a great place to look because most items include sample scripts, which can be run independently so that you can see the results immediately.

  □ The *Object Scripting* index contains a list of objects and the messages that are available for each object. For example, suppose you wanted to add a column to a data table. From this index, you can click **Data Table** on the left then scroll through the list of possibilities on the right. Approximately half way through the list, you will find **New Column**. You could then go back to the *JSL Functions* index and look up **New Column** to find the syntax and sample script, as mentioned previously.

  □ The *DisplayBox Scripting* index is similar to the *Object Scripting* index. As you read in Chapter Three, this index contains a list of display boxes and the corresponding messages that are available for each.

- **Show Properties:** You can also run a **Show Properties** command with the object. This command provides the same information as listed in the *Object Scripting* index mentioned previously. Here is the basic syntax—notice that the object (or a reference to the object) you are working with is used as the argument:

  ```
  Show Properties( object );
  ```

- *JMP Scripting Guide*: As you probably have already found, the *JMP Scripting Guide* is full of information. We think it is a great reference manual for scripters who have a little prior experience. While printed versions of the manual are no longer shipped with JMP, the PDF version is available from within JMP by selecting the **Help** menu and selecting **Books ▶ JMP Scripting Guide**. Because the PDF version can be searched very easily, this could become your preferred method for using the guide.

- **JMPfile exchange:** The *JMPfile exchange*, which is located in the *User Community* section of the JMP Web site (http://www.jmp.com) offers a location for JMP users to exchange JMP scripts. If there is a particular problem you are trying to address or if you have written a script that you want to share, you might want to check out this site.

What To Do in Times of Trouble

After executing a script, you might find yourself facing unexpected results or error messages in the log. What went wrong and, more importantly, how do you fix it?

While it is impossible to give you a list of all the possible error messages and what to do about each, we can offer some advice based upon years of helping people with their scripting questions.

Common Issues

First, let's go over some common issues. These are issues that seem to stand out as being common among scripters, regardless of experience level:

- Current Data Table: Different Than Expected
- Timing Issues: When Tasks Are Not Yet Completed

Current Data Table: Different Than Expected

When multiple data tables are opened and closed during the processing of a script, how do you know which data table is the current data table? Though you might think JMP is looking at one table, often JMP is looking at another table. Therefore, it is best for your script to be data table specific. This is even more important when you have multiple tables that have the same column names.

So how can we deal with this?

One solution is to specify the current data table with a **Current Data Table** command. The reference to the data table is used as its argument. For example, when **dt** is the name (or reference) you have assigned to a specific data table,

```
dt = Data Table( "Big Class" );
```

then you would use **dt** as the argument for the **Current Data Table** command:

```
Current Data Table( dt );
```

This makes it clear to JMP which data table should be the current, or active, data table.

To specify the data table that should be used for an analysis, send the analysis platform message to a specific data table:

```
dt << Distribution( Nominal Distribution( Column( :age ) ) );
```

This way, JMP knows it will find the **age** column in the data table referenced by **dt**.

When you have multiple data tables open that contain some of the same column names, you can use the **Column** statement with the optional data table reference. This tells JMP exactly which table to look in for a column by the name specified in the second argument.

You can use the **Column** statement in the following ways:

- Specify the actual column name in double quotation marks
  ```
  Column( dt, "age" );
  ```
- Specify the column number
  ```
  Column( dt, 2 );
  ```
- Specify the column name stored in a variable
  ```
  var = "age";
  Column( dt, var );
  ```

Often, people use the **dt:column** syntax for this purpose. While this might be appropriate in some instances, it is important to understand that this syntax is actually a *column variable* rather than a *column reference*.

So what's the difference? A *column variable* is a scoping operator, which requires a row number in order to return a value. If the current row is not set, then a missing value will be returned. This is because the current row is always zero unless specified otherwise. Other column variables include **As Column(dt, column)** and the **:column** syntax.

A *column reference* is a reference to the column in its entirety, as one unit. A *column reference* can also be subscripted to refer to a particular value within a column. The

Column statement is an example of a *column reference.* Yet, it can act as a *column variable* when it is subscripted, as in the following example:

```
Column( dt, "age" )[2];
```

Timing Issues: When Tasks Are Not Yet Completed

JMP considers certain tasks as system-related and performs them in the background. Some of these tasks are:

- Formula evaluation

- Closing data tables

- Screen updates

While updating contents of a screen, most likely, would not cause you trouble, incomplete formula evaluation or delayed data table closing, most definitely, can cause you trouble.

For example, suppose your script adds a column that contains a formula, and then immediately creates a Summary table. If the formula has not completely evaluated prior to creating the Summary table, a JMP error alert will appear, indicating the data has changed, and your script will halt execution.

The **Run Formulas** command forces all formulas in a data table to evaluate completely before the next JSL statement can be executed. The syntax for **Run Formulas** is as follows:

```
dt << Run Formulas;
```

Beginning with JMP 6, all analysis platforms automatically send a **Run Formulas** command to the data table prior to performing the analysis. This is to ensure the analysis will not be performed on any columns that have incomplete data.

However, this is not the case with any of the Tables menu commands. In the example mentioned previously, where the script added a column with a formula and then created a Summary table, it would be wise to include a **Run Formulas** statement immediately after adding the column and prior to referencing the data table for the purpose of creating the Summary table. This ensures the column is completely populated before the Summary table is produced.

Figure 4.4 Run Formulas

```
Script
1    dt = Data Table( "Big Class.jmp" );
2
3    dt << New Column( "Grade",
4         Numeric,
5         Continuous,
6         Format( "Best", 10 ),
7         Formula( Match( :age, 12, 6, 13, 7, 14, 8, 15, 9, 16, 10, 17, 11 ) )
8    );
9
10   dt << Run Formulas;
11
12   dt << Summary( Group( :Grade ), Mean( :height ) );
```

Another way to address timing issues is to include **Wait** statements. Adding a **Wait** statement allows time so that pending system-related tasks have an opportunity to complete.

When opening and closing data tables within a **For** loop, it is possible for the actual closing of a data table to occur later than you expect. This is because closing data tables is one of those tasks JMP performs in the background.

In instances such as this, adding a **Wait** statement with a short period of time (in number of seconds) as the argument might give just enough time to complete the closing of the data table before moving on to the next task:

```
Wait(0.1);
```

We recommend starting with a small amount of time and increasing in very small increments only if necessary.

Debugging Tips

Script with Style!
If you choose not to use the Script Editor's automatic formatting feature, adopt a method of formatting your code for readability. Some things to consider are:

- Use consistent naming conventions
- Include comments

- Use indentions
- Skip lines

Commenting and formatting your script is not only helpful for debugging, but also for quickly identifying sections of code you might want to copy and use in a future scripting project.

To easily recognize variable names, begin each variable name with a lowercase letter using CamelCase for multiple words. Conversely, begin each JSL command with an uppercase letter. These are suggestions only and are not required by JMP.

Keep It Simple!

Build the script in small sections, running each section of code independently to verify its success before moving on to the next section.

If **For** loops are included, be sure to run the code within the loop to ensure it will run successfully for each iteration of the loop.

You can run an entire script at once. Or to see results of an individual section, just highlight the desired section of code and use one of the methods mentioned previously to run it. Another way to run the highlighted code is to press the **ENTER** key on the numeric keypad.

Check the Log.

Was there an error message or were the results not what you expected?

First, check the log for messages, paying close attention to any specific line numbers where an error was encountered. To go directly to the line in your script where the error occurred, from the **Edit** menu, select **Go to Line**. You will then be prompted to enter a line number. This will move your cursor to the line number that you specified.

If no line numbers are included in the log message, the message itself should give you some clue about what JMP did not understand or know how to process. Some common mistakes that people make are to have unequal fences or to forget a semicolon. The error messages generated for these items are generally very specific. However, if you include an extraneous comma, the problem can be quite a bit harder to find—even for an experienced scripter.

Isolate the Problem.

Attempt to narrow down where the problem originated. Some suggestions are:

- Run the script line by line or in small sections until it produces the undesired results.

- Run the code within any **For** loops to verify that the entire loop can be executed successfully.

- Check the values for any variables that are mentioned in and around error messages.

- Use a **Show** command at various points in your script to display variable values as your script runs. Here is the syntax for the **Show** command:

  ```
  Show( dt );
  ```

After the script has been executed, hover your mouse over a global variable in the Script window. JMP will display the current value of that variable. This is another helpful feature of the Script Editor!

Is There a Better Way?

Ask yourself if there is a simpler way to accomplish the same goal. For example, if you just need to know how many levels there are in a column, don't create a whole Summary table that only groups by the desired column. Instead, use the **Summarize** command to get a list of the levels and use the **N Items()** function to find out how many levels there are. Using the **Summarize** command prevents the creation of a data table that must be managed, uses less memory, and is faster, while providing the same information.

A sample script that uses the **Summarize** command is included in Section 2: Jump On!

Or, suppose you need to know how many rows were selected as the result of a Select Where command. What would you do? You could loop through each row, check the row state of each row, and keep a count of those rows that had a selected row state. But a better solution would be to capture a matrix of the row numbers that are selected using the **Get Selected Rows** command, and then find out the number of rows in the matrix.

So instead of code like this:

```
c = 0;
For Each Row(
   If( Selected( Row State() ), c++ )
);
```

Your code would look much more concise and be much faster:

```
selRows = N Row( dt << Get Selected Rows );
```

Summary

Now you are ready to get your scripting projects started. You know how to make JMP do a lot of the work for you. You know where to get help. And you know what steps to take to debug a problem. There's no stopping you now!

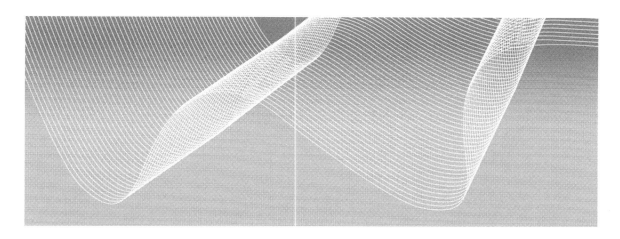

Section 2

Jump On!

After learning the basics, you are ready to think about specific tasks you want to accomplish using JMP scripting. Typically, when users contact JMP Technical Support with scripting questions, the questions are in the form of, "How do I do *this* or *that* in a script?" Or, "I need an example that shows me the syntax to get *this* done."

Therefore, we have dedicated this section of the book to those of you who want to find a good example on how to do something in JSL. Here, you will find over fifty examples on a variety of topics that are divided into five categories:

- Rows, Columns, and Tables
- Dialog Windows
- Analyses
- Changing Graph Axes
- Reports and Journals

Each example answers a question with a script sample, including embedded explanatory comments. In addition, many examples include a discussion section to explain functions in detail or give helpful references. These script samples can be copied and pasted into a script window and executed immediately using sample data tables to show you exactly how the solution works.

As you look through the examples, you will notice gray boxes in the code. These boxes are meant to highlight the portion of the script that is most important. Script code that is not included in a gray box is there to set up the script to be a complete example.

There might be multiple ways to accomplish the same task. The methods we use assume that you are a beginning scripter and thus, few advanced methods are demonstrated. As you become more proficient in your scripting, we encourage you to experiment with your code.

Enjoy!

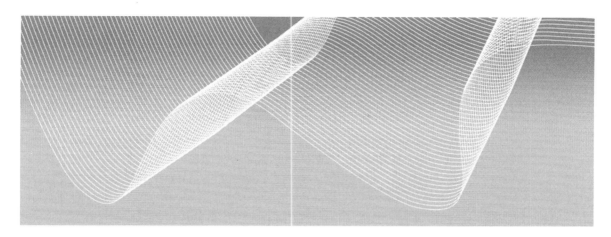

C h a p t e r   F i v e

Rows, Columns, and Tables

Questions

Question 5.1:

I can manipulate a data table interactively, such as by selecting and deleting rows, by adding new columns, etc. How can I get JMP to produce the script for these actions?

Solution 5.1:

As we mentioned in Chapter One, JMP does not record your steps. It can, however, reproduce the data table in its current state using the **Get Script** command:

```
Current Data Table() << Get Script;
```

Note: The result of running the previous code will be pasted in the log. You can copy the New Table command from the log and paste it into your main script.

If you have only a few manipulations, it might be easier to write the code yourself for the desired manipulation. The following code demonstrates how to do a few of the table manipulations mentioned previously. Further details can be found in the "Data Tables" chapter of the *JMP Scripting Guide*.

```
/* Open the sample data table, Big Class.  */
dt = Open( "$SAMPLE_DATA/Big Class.jmp" );

/* Select rows where the age is 16 or greater. */
dt << Select Where( :age >= 16 );

/* Delete the selected rows. */
dt << Delete Rows;

/* Add a column containing the column mean of height. */
dt << New Column( "Mean Height",
   Numeric,
   Continuous,
   Formula( Col Mean( :height ) )
);
```

Note: To run this script, go to **support.sas.com/jumpintojmp** and select **Solution 5.1**. Copy and paste the code into a new Script window, and then select **Edit ▶ Run Script** to see the results.

Result 5.1:

The resulting data table should have 34 rows and 6 columns, as shown in Figure 5.1.

Figure 5.1 Data Table After Deleting Rows and Adding a Formula Column

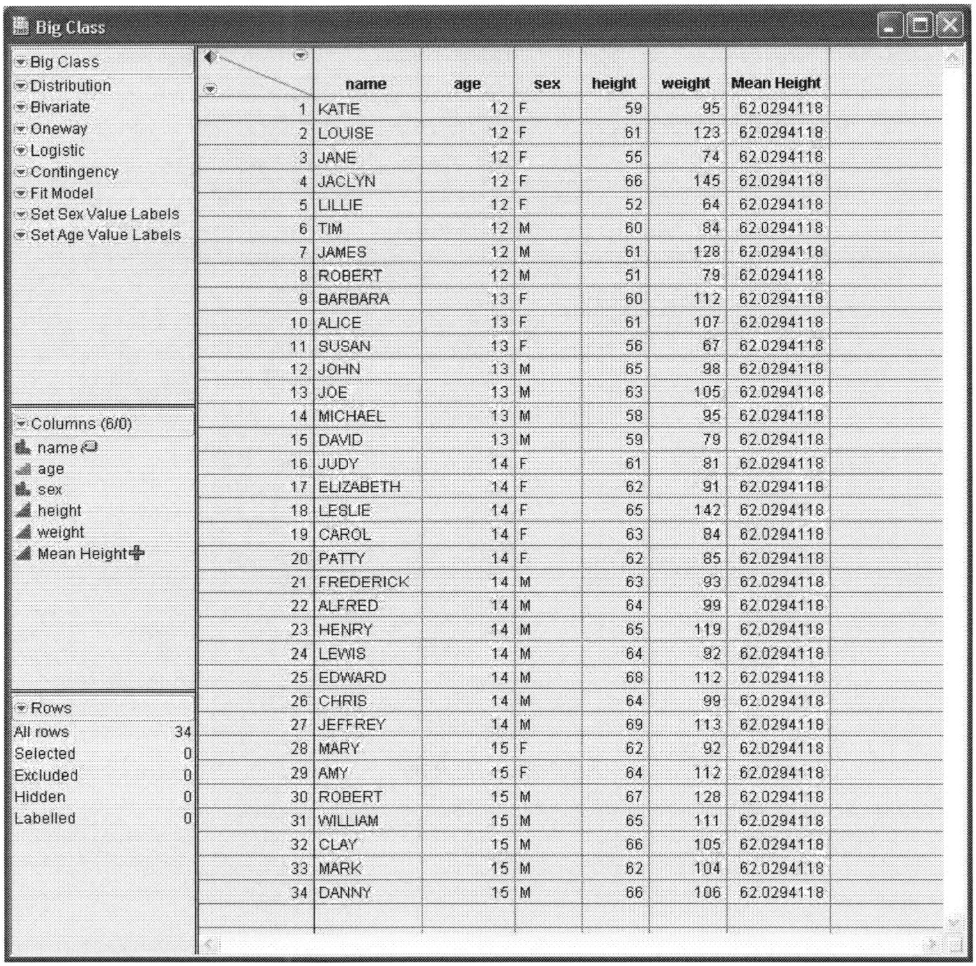

	name	age	sex	height	weight	Mean Height
1	KATIE	12	F	59	95	62.0294118
2	LOUISE	12	F	61	123	62.0294118
3	JANE	12	F	55	74	62.0294118
4	JACLYN	12	F	66	145	62.0294118
5	LILLIE	12	F	52	64	62.0294118
6	TIM	12	M	60	84	62.0294118
7	JAMES	12	M	61	128	62.0294118
8	ROBERT	12	M	51	79	62.0294118
9	BARBARA	13	F	60	112	62.0294118
10	ALICE	13	F	61	107	62.0294118
11	SUSAN	13	F	56	67	62.0294118
12	JOHN	13	M	65	98	62.0294118
13	JOE	13	M	63	105	62.0294118
14	MICHAEL	13	M	58	95	62.0294118
15	DAVID	13	M	59	79	62.0294118
16	JUDY	14	F	61	81	62.0294118
17	ELIZABETH	14	F	62	91	62.0294118
18	LESLIE	14	F	65	142	62.0294118
19	CAROL	14	F	63	84	62.0294118
20	PATTY	14	F	62	85	62.0294118
21	FREDERICK	14	M	63	93	62.0294118
22	ALFRED	14	M	64	99	62.0294118
23	HENRY	14	M	65	119	62.0294118
24	LEWIS	14	M	64	92	62.0294118
25	EDWARD	14	M	68	112	62.0294118
26	CHRIS	14	M	64	99	62.0294118
27	JEFFREY	14	M	69	113	62.0294118
28	MARY	15	F	62	92	62.0294118
29	AMY	15	F	64	112	62.0294118
30	ROBERT	15	M	67	128	62.0294118
31	WILLIAM	15	M	65	111	62.0294118
32	CLAY	15	M	66	105	62.0294118
33	MARK	15	M	62	104	62.0294118
34	DANNY	15	M	66	106	62.0294118

Question 5.2:

How can I select rows where more than one condition is true? How can I select rows where at least one of the specified conditions is true?

Solution 5.2:

Use the logical operator AND or '&' to select within a selection as shown in the following code:

```
/* Open the sample data table, Big Class.jmp. */
dt = Open( "$SAMPLE_DATA/Big Class.jmp" );
```

```
dt << Select Where( :age > 14 & :height < 65 );
```

Use the logical operator OR or '|' to extend a selection:

```
dt << Select Where( :age > 14 | :height > 65 );
```

Note: To run this script, go to **support.sas.com/jumpintojmp** and select **Solution 5.2**. Copy and paste the code into a new Script window, and then select **Edit ▶ Run Script** to see the results.

Result 5.2:

The following images show the results of using the '&' and '|' operators for selecting rows.

Figure 5.2 Row Selection where Age > 14 and Height < 65

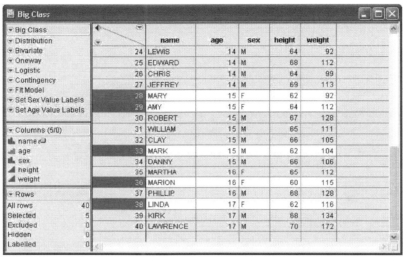

Figure 5.3 Row Selection where Age > 14 or Height > 65

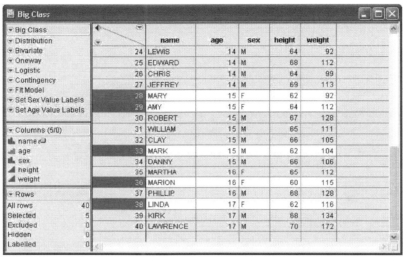

Question 5.3:

How can I perform a Select Where on dates?

Solution 5.3:

In order to select rows that contain date or time values, you will need to use the **Informat** function with the appropriate format as shown in the following code:

```
/* Open the sample data table, Abrasion.jmp. */
dt = Open( "$SAMPLE_DATA/Abrasion.jmp" );
```

```
/* Use the Informat function to convert the string datetime
   value to a JMP date value. */
dt << Select Where(
    :Date >= Informat( "4/30/1995 12:00:00 PM", "m/d/y h:m:s" )
    &
    :Date <= Informat( "5/01/1995 12:00:00 PM", "m/d/y h:m:s" )
);
```

Note: To run this script, go to **support.sas.com/jumpintojmp** and select **Solution 5.3**. Copy and paste the code into a new Script window, and then select **Edit ▶ Run Script** to see the results.

Discussion 5.3:

The **Informat** function converts a date or date time character string (specified in the first argument) into a JMP date value, which is the number of seconds since January 1, 1904. It is this numeric value that JMP needs for the comparison in **Select Where**. This example assumes that the forward slash, '/', is used as the date separator.

For more information on the **Informat** function, click **Help ▶ Indexes ▶ JSL Operators** or **Functions** (depending upon your release of JMP), browse to **Informat**, and then select **Informat**.

Result 5.3

Figure 5.4 Rows Selected within Specified Date Criteria

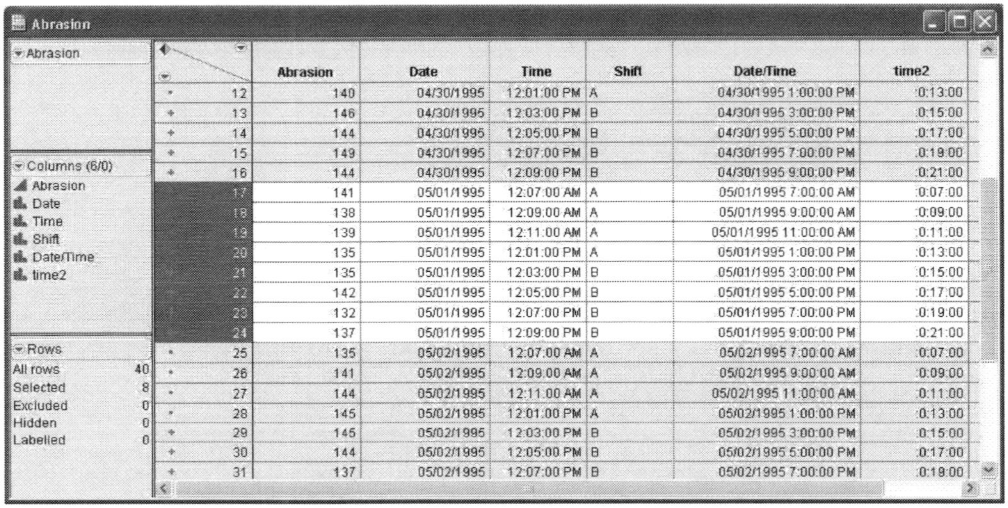

Question 5.4:

How can I determine the number of selected, excluded, or hidden rows in a data table?

Solution 5.4:

Use the **Get Selected Rows**, **Get Excluded Rows**, and **Get Hidden Rows** commands to obtain a matrix of row numbers, and then use the **N Row()** function to obtain the number of rows in the matrix as shown in the following code:

```
/* Open the sample data table, Fitness.jmp. */
dt = Open( "$SAMPLE_DATA/Fitness.jmp" );

/* Select, exclude, and hide some rows for demonstration
purposes */
dt << Select Where( :age <= 40 ) << Exclude( 1 ) << Hide( 1 );

selRows = N Row( dt << Get Selected Rows );

exclRows = N Row( dt << Get Excluded Rows );

hidnRows = N Row( dt << Get Hidden Rows );

/* Print variable values in the log. */
Show( selRows, exclRows, hidnRows );
```

Note: To run this script, go to **support.sas.com/jumpintojmp** and select **Solution 5.4**. Copy and paste the code into a new Script window, and then select **Edit ▶ Run Script** to see the results.

Discussion 5.4:

While the **Get Selected Rows** command has been available in earlier versions of JMP, the **Get Excluded Rows** and **Get Hidden Rows** commands are new to JMP 8. See the next example to learn how to get the number of excluded and hidden rows in releases prior to JMP 8.

Result 5.4:

The example script assumes the current data table contains rows that are selected, excluded, and hidden. Figure 5.5 shows the result posted in the log.

Figure 5.5 Log After Script Was Executed

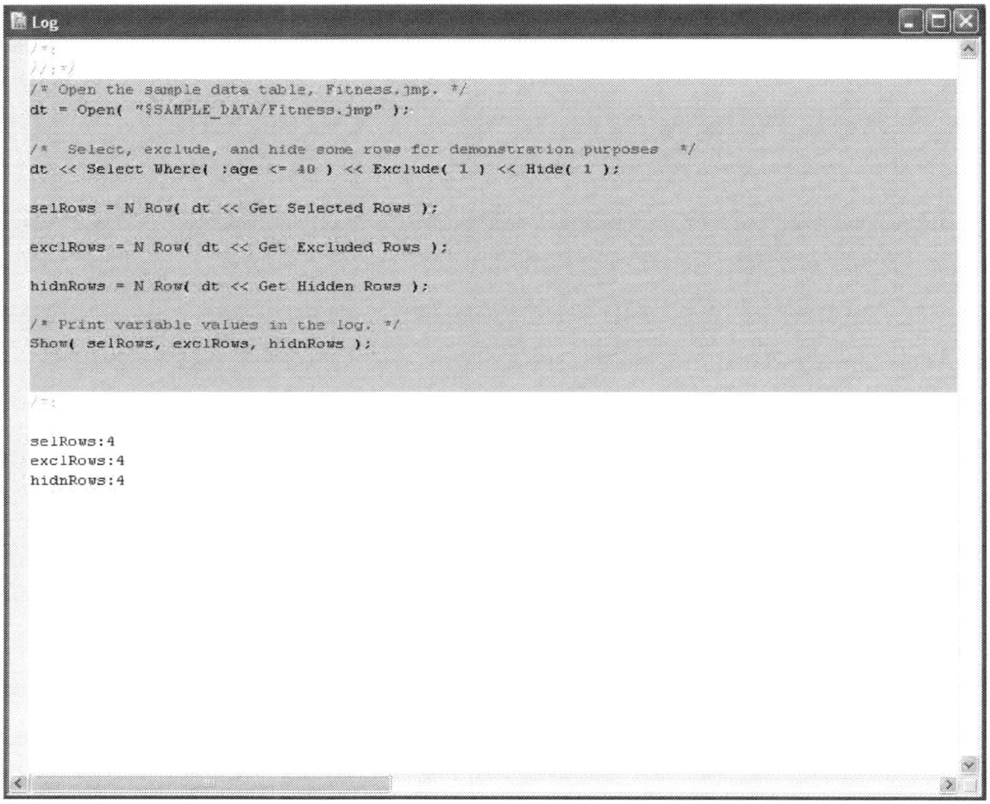

Question 5.5:

I'm using a release of JMP prior to JMP 8. How can I get the number of hidden and excluded rows in a data table?

Solution 5.5:

Use the **Select Excluded** and **Select Hidden** messages for the data table as shown in the following code:

```
/* Open the sample data table, Fitness.jmp. */
dt = Open( "$SAMPLE_DATA/Fitness.jmp" );

/*  Select, exclude, and hide some rows for demonstration
purposes  */
dt << Select Where( :age <= 40 ) << Exclude( 1 ) << Hide( 1 );
dt << Clear Select;

/* Select excluded rows then count with Get Selected Rows. */
dt << Select Excluded;
exclRows = N Row( dt << Get Selected Rows );

/* Select hidden rows then count with Get Selected Rows. */
dt << Select Hidden;
hidnRows = N Row( dt << Get Selected Rows );

/* Print variable values in the log. */
Show( exclRows, hidnRows );
```

Note: To run this script, go to **support.sas.com/jumpintojmp** and select **Solution 5.5**. Copy and paste the code into a new Script window, and then select **Edit ▶ Run Script** to see the results.

Discussion 5.5:

If you just want the number of selected rows, the code would look the same as it did in the previous example:

```
selRows = N Row( dt << Get Selected Rows );
```

Result 5.5:

The example script assumes the current data table contains rows that are selected, excluded, and hidden. Figure 5.6 shows the result posted in the log.

Figure 5.6 Log After Script Was Executed

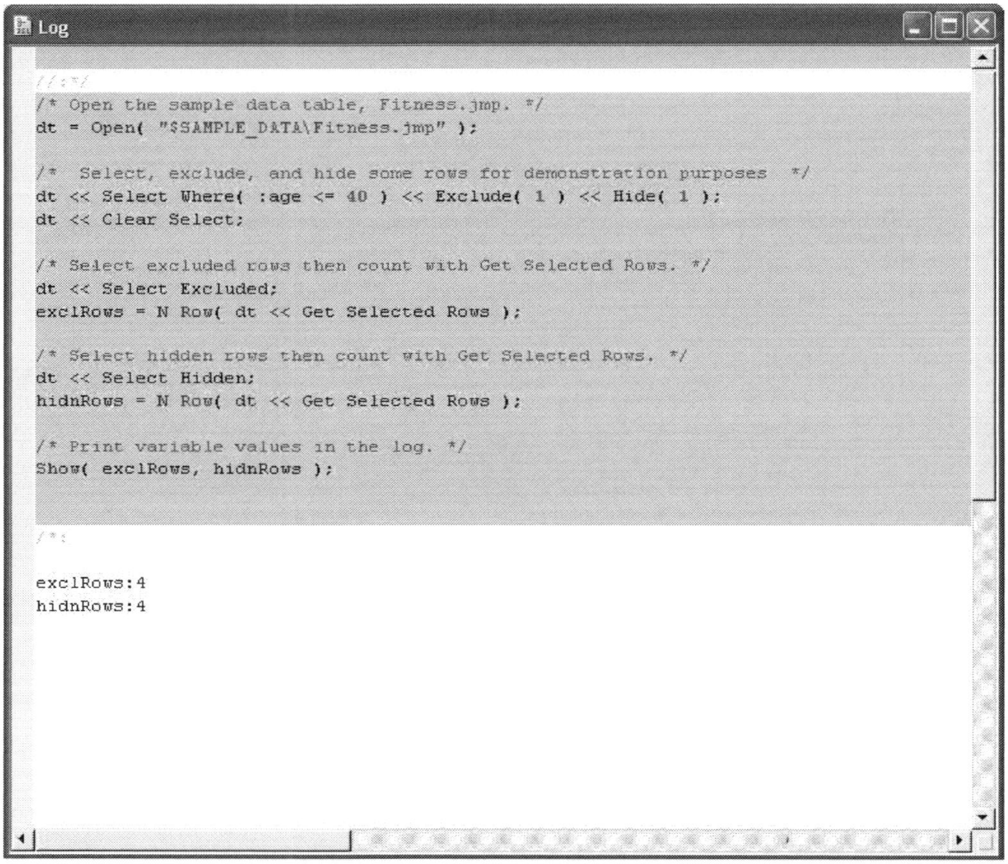

```
/* ; */
/* Open the sample data table, Fitness.jmp. */
dt = Open( "$SAMPLE_DATA\Fitness.jmp" );

/*  Select, exclude, and hide some rows for demonstration purposes  */
dt << Select Where( :age <= 40 ) << Exclude( 1 ) << Hide( 1 );
dt << Clear Select;

/* Select excluded rows then count with Get Selected Rows. */
dt << Select Excluded;
exclRows = N Row( dt << Get Selected Rows );

/* Select hidden rows then count with Get Selected Rows. */
dt << Select Hidden;
hidnRows = N Row( dt << Get Selected Rows );

/* Print variable values in the log. */
Show( exclRows, hidnRows );


/* ;

exclRows:4
hidnRows:4
```

Question 5.6:

I am attempting to select some rows, and then create a subset data table. When no rows are selected, all the rows are included in the subset data table. How can I create a subset only if there were rows selected?

Solution 5.6:

Get the number of rows selected using the **Get Selected Rows** command, and then verify the result is greater than 0 before creating the subset as shown in the following code:

```
/* Open the Big Class sample data table. */
dt = Open( "$SAMPLE_DATA/Fitness.jmp" );

/* Select the desired rows. */
dt << Select Where( :age == 54 & :sex == "F" );

/* Store the number of selected rows in a global variable. */
selRows = N Row( dt << Get Selected Rows );

/* Perform a subset if rows were selected. Otherwise, print
   a message in the log. */
If( selRows > 0,
    dt << Subset( Output Table Name( "Age 54 Females" ) ),
    Print("No rows selected.")
);
```

Note: To run this script, go to **support.sas.com/jumpintojmp** and select **Solution 5.6**. Copy and paste the code into a new Script window, and then select **Edit ▶ Run Script** to see the results.

Discussion 5.6:

Because the Fitness sample data table does not contain any rows that meet the criteria specified in the Select Where statement, the statement No rows selected will be printed in the log upon running the script.

Question 5.7:

How can I determine the number of selected columns in a table? How can I get a list of the selected columns?

Solution 5.7:

Use the **Get Selected Columns** command to obtain a list of column names, and then use the **N Items()** function to obtain the number of selected columns in the list as shown in the following code:

```
/*  Open a sample data table for demonstration purposes.  */
dt = Open( "$SAMPLE_DATA/Big Class.JMP" );

/* Select the first two columns for demonstration purposes. */
Column( 1 ) << Set Selected;
Column( 2 ) << Set Selected;

/* Store the list of selected columns in a variable. */
selColList = dt << Get Selected Columns;

/* Store the number of items in the list in a variable. */
numSelCols = N Items( selColList );

/* Show variable values in the log. */
Show( selColList, numSelCols );
```

Note: To run this script, go to **support.sas.com/jumpintojmp** and select **Solution 5.7**. Copy and paste the code into a new Script window, and then select **Edit ▶ Run Script** to see the results.

Question 5.8:

Are there any JSL commands for recoding data, as in **Cols ▶ Recode**?

Solution 5.8:

Currently, there are no JSL commands for **Recode** from the **Cols** menu. Therefore, you must write JSL code that effectively performs the same function.

```
/* Create a new data table. */
dt = New Table( "City Data",
    Add Rows( 10 ),
    New Column( "US Cities",
        Character,
        Nominal,
        Set Values(
            {"NEW YORK CITY", " LOS ANGELES", "  CHICAGO   ",
             "HOUSTON", "PHOENIX", "PHILADELPHIA       ",
             " SAN  ANTONIO ", "SAN     DIEGO ", "DALLAS",
             "  SAN   JOSE  "}
        )
    ),
    New Column( "State",
        Character,
        Nominal,
        Set Values(
            {"NEW YORK", "CALIFORNIA", "ILLINOIS", "TEXAS",
             "ARIZONA", "PENNSYLVANIA", "TEXAS", "CALIFORNIA",
             "TEXAS", "CALIFORNIA"}
        )
    )
);

Wait( 1 ); //For demonstration purposes.
```

```
/* Titlecase - In Place */
For Each Row(
    /* Make each value lowercase. */
    :State = Lowercase( :State );
    /* Capture a list of all the words in the string. */
    wrds = Words( :State, " " );
    /* Loop through each word, capitalizing the first letter.
*/
```

```
    For( i = 1, i <= N Items( wrds ), i++,
        wrds[i] = Munger( wrds[i], 1, 1,
                        Uppercase( Substr( wrds[i], 1, 1 ) ) );
        If( i > 1,
            newVal = newVal || " ",
            newVal = ""
        );
        newVal = newVal || wrds[i];
    );
    /* Assign the Titlecase value. */
    :State = newVal;
);
```

```
Wait( 1 ); //For demonstration purposes.
```

```
/* Uppercase/Lowercase - In Formula Column*/
dt << New Column( "State Case",
    Character,
    /* Move comment characters for desired case */
    Formula(
        Uppercase( :State )
      //Lowercase( :State )
    )
);
```

```
Wait( 1 ); //For demonstration purposes.
```

```
/* Trim and Collapse Whitespace - In New Column */
/* Add a new column. */
dt << New Column( "Trimmed Cities", Character );

For Each Row(
    /* Capture a list of all the words in the string. */
    wrds = Words( :US Cities, " " );
    /* Loop through each word, concatenating the values
       with a single space between each. */
    For( i = 1, i <= N Items( wrds ), i++,
        If( i == 1,
            newVal = "",
            newVal = newVal || " "
        );
        newVal = newVal || wrds[i];
    );
    /* Assign the trimmed value to the new column. */
    :Trimmed Cities = newVal;
);
```

```
Wait( 1 ); //For demonstration purposes.

/* Specify new recode values in a formula column. */
dt << New Column( "State Abbr.",
    Character,
    Formula(
        Match( :State,
            "New York", "NY",
            "California", "CA",
            "Illinois", "IL",
            "Texas", "TX",
            "Arizona", "AZ",
            "Pennsylvania", "PA"
        )
    )
);
```

Note: To run this script, go to **support.sas.com/jumpintojmp** and select **Solution 5.8**. Copy and paste the code into a new Script window, and then select **Edit ▶ Run Script** to see the results.

Discussion 5.8:

In Recode, there are five options on the red triangle for recoding the data:

- Convert to Titlecase
- Convert to Uppercase
- Convert to Lowercase
- Trim Whitespace
- Collapse Whitespace

There are three locations for storing the recoded data:

- In Place
- In New Column
- In Formula Column

Additionally, you can specify different values.

The previous four examples demonstrate each option for recoding the data and identify each of the locations for storing the recoded data. The example for Trim Whitespace is combined with Collapse Whitespace because the same script will accomplish both tasks.

Question 5.9:

I want to delete all the character columns in a table. How can I do this?

Solution 5.9:

Use the **Get Column Names** function with a Character argument to obtain a list of all character columns in the table. Use **Delete Columns** to delete all columns named in the list.

```
/* Open the sample data table, Big Class.jmp. */
dt = Open( "$SAMPLE_DATA/Big Class.jmp" );

/* Store all the character column names in a list. */
cols = dt << Get Column Names( Character );

/* Delete the columns. */
dt << Delete Columns( cols );
```

Note: To run this script, go to **support.sas.com/jumpintojmp** and select **Solution 5.9**. Copy and paste the code into a new Script window, and then select **Edit ▶ Run Script** to see the results.

Question 5.10:

How can I delete the formula from every column in my data table?

Solution 5.10:

Get the formula using the **Get Property** command and delete the formula property if present, as shown in the following code:

```
/* Open the IRLS Example sample data table. */
dt = Open( "$SAMPLE_DATA/Nonlinear Examples/IRLS Example.jmp"
);
```

```
/* Loop through each column in the data table. */
For( i = 1, i <= N Col( dt ), i++,
/* Obtain the formula column property. */
   fmla = Column( dt, i ) << Get Property( "Formula" );
/* Delete the formula, if one exists. */
   If( Type( Name Expr( fmla ) ) == "Expression",
        Column( dt, i ) << Delete Formula
   );
);
```

Note: To run this script, go to **support.sas.com/jumpintojmp** and select **Solution 5.10**. Copy and paste the code into a new Script window, and then select **Edit ▶ Run Script** to see the results.

Question 5.11:

I have a list of values that I need to use as the only possible values for a column. How can I pass this list to the List Check column property?

Solution 5.11:

Use **Eval Expr**() to resolve the list variable prior to evaluation of **Set Property**():

```
/*  Open a sample data table for demonstration purposes.  */
dt = Open( "$SAMPLE_DATA/Big Class.JMP" );

/*  Create the list of values to be used in the List Check.  */
genderList = {"M", "F"};

/*  Create a reference to the desired column.  */
col = Column( dt, "sex" );
```

```
/*  Create an expression within an expression.  */
listCkExpr = Expr( col << Set Property(
  "List Check",
  Expr( genderList )
  )
);

/*  Resolve the main expression.  */
Eval(
  /*  Resolve the global variable expression.  */
  Eval Expr( listCkExpr )
);
```

Note: To run this script, go to **support.sas.com/jumpintojmp** and select **Solution 5.11**. Copy and paste the code into a new Script window, and then select **Edit ▶ Run Script** to see the results.

Discussion 5.11:

To add the **List Check** column property, you would use the **Set Property** command with the name of the column property and a list of values as its argument. To use a variable in place of the list in the argument, we set the entire **Set Property** statement as an expression by wrapping it with the **Expr()** function. Further, we identify the variable by wrapping it in a second expression; thereby, creating an expression within an expression.

The **Eval Expr()** function causes the variable within the main expression to be resolved. Finally, the main expression is evaluated using the **Eval()** function.

Result 5.11:

Figure 5.7 List Check Column Property Added to Column

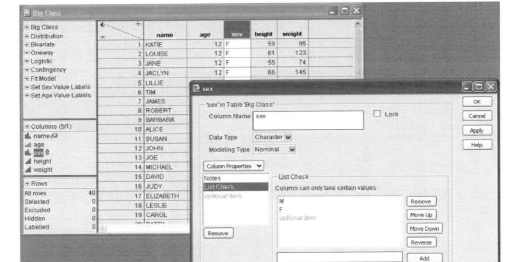

Question 5.12:

I am trying to prompt the user for information, and then use the responses in a column formula. How can I use a variable in a column formula?

Solution 5.12:

When using variables in formulas, the variable name should be replaced with its value before it is assigned to the formula as shown in the following code:

```
/* Prompt the user for information in a Dialog. */
dlg = Dialog( "BMI Calculator",
    Vlist(
        TextBox( "      " ),
        Hlist(
            TextBox( "Enter your Height (in inches):   " ),
            ht = EditNumber( 0 )
        ),
        TextBox( "      " ),
        Hlist(
            TextBox( "Enter your Weight (in pounds):   " ),
            wt = EditNumber( 0 )
        ),
        TextBox( "      " )
    )
);

/* Extract the values to be used in the formula. */
yourHt = dlg["ht"];
yourWt = dlg["wt"];

/* Create a new table to store the results. */
nt = New Table( "Your BMI",
    New Column( "Date",
                Numeric,
                Continuous,
                Format( "m/d/y", 10 ),
                Formula( Today() ) ),
    New Column( "BMI", Numeric, Continuous ),
    New Column( "Range",
                Character,
                Formula(
                    If(
                        :BMI < 18.5, "Underweight",
                        18.5 <= :BMI < 25, "Normal",
```

```
                            25 <= :BMI < 30, "Overweight",
                            :BMI > 30, "Obese" ) ) ),
        Add Rows( 1 )
);
```

```
/* Build the main expression that will add the formula. */
formulaExpr = Expr(
    /* Identify the global variables which must be resolved
        first. */
    Column( "BMI" ) << Formula(
            Expr( yourWt ) / ( Expr( yourHt ) ^ 2 ) * 703 )
);

/* Resolve the main expression. */
Eval(
    /* Resolve the global variable expression. */
    Eval Expr( formulaExpr )
);
```

Note: To run this script, go to **support.sas.com/jumpintojmp** and select **Solution 5.12**. Copy and paste the code into a new Script window, and then select **Edit ▶ Run Script** to see the results.

Discussion 5.12:

If you do not replace the global variable with its value in the formula, the result of the formula can change each time the value of the global variable changes.

Question 5.13:

I can replace all the missing numeric values in a table with zeros interactively by performing **Edit ▶ Search ▶ Find and Replace**. How can I do the same procedure using scripting?

Solution 5.13:

Use two **For** loops to traverse the table, one for columns and the other for rows, checking each cell in the numeric columns. If a value is found missing, the missing value symbol is replaced with a zero.

```
/* Open the sample data table, Cities.jmp. */
dt = Open("$SAMPLE_DATA/Cities.jmp");
```

```
/* Obtain a list of all numeric column names as strings.  */
numCols = dt << Get Column Names( Numeric, String );

/* Loop through each numeric column.  */
For( i = 1, i <= N Items( numCols ), i++,
/* Loop through each row.  */
    For( j = 1, j <= N Rows( dt ), j++,
/* The IsMissing function will return a '1' or true if the
value is missing.  If true, cell is assigned zero. */
        If( Is Missing( Column( dt, numCols[i] )[j] ),
            Column( dt, numCols[i] )[j] = 0
        )
    )
);
```

Note: To run this script, go to **support.sas.com/jumpintojmp** and select **Solution 5.13**. Copy and paste the code into a new Script window, and then select **Edit ▶ Run Script** to see the results.

Question 5.14:

How can I get a list of all open data tables?

Solution 5.14:

Use a **For** loop to access each table name, and then insert each name into a list:

```
/* Initialize an empty list where the table names will be
   stored. */
dtNames = {};
```

```
/* Loop through each open data table and insert its
   name into the list. */
For( i = 1, i <= N Table(), i++,
    Insert Into( dtNames, Data Table( i ) << Get Name )
);
```

```
/* Print names in the log. */
Show( dtNames );
```

Note: To run this script, go to **support.sas.com/jumpintojmp** and select **Solution 5.14**. Copy and paste the code into a new Script window, and then select **Edit ▶ Run Script** to see the results.

Discussion 5.14:

The **N Table()** function returns the number of tables open. The **Get Name** command returns the name of the data table. **Insert Into** inserts the value in the second argument (the data table name, in this example) into the list specified in the first argument.

Question 5.15:

How can I close all open data tables without saving any of them?

Solution 5.15:

Use a **For** loop to access each table, and then issue the **Close()** command:

```
/*  Assign the number of open data tables to a variable  */
numTables = N Table();
```

```
/*  Issue the Close statement once for each of the open
    Data tables in a For loop  */
For( i = 1, i <= numTables, i++,
    Close( Data Table( 1 ), No Save );
    Wait( 0 );   //Needed for releases prior to JMP 7 only
);
```

```
Show( N Table() );
```

Note: To run this script, go to **support.sas.com/jumpintojmp** and select **Solution 5.15**. Copy and paste the code into a new Script window, and then select **Edit ▶ Run Script** to see the results.

Discussion 5.15:

In this example, we used the variable *numTables* in the *whileExpr* argument of the **For** loop. If we had used the **N Table()** function instead, not all the tables would be closed. Why? Because the number of open tables is always decreasing and *i* is always increasing. Therefore, at some point the number of open tables would be less than *i*, so the loop would stop.

Beginning with JMP 8, a new command was added that will allow the script author to close all data tables, reports, or journals without saving them. This new command is **Close All**. If the script will be executed by users of various versions of JMP, the above method is best. Here is the syntax for **Close All**:

```
Close All( Data Tables, No Save );
Close All( Reports, No Save);
Close All( Journals, No Save);
```

Question 5.16:

How can I open and concatenate multiple files that have the same format?

Solution 5.16:

Loop through a list of the filenames and concatenate each file into a main table as shown in the following code:

```
/* Create a list of all the files to be concatenated. */
myFiles = {"Fat Content.jmp", "Total Carbohydrates.jmp",
    "Nutrients.jmp"};
```

```
/* Loop through each file */
For( i = 1, i <= N Items( myFiles ), i++,
    /* If the file is the first in the list, open it.
        Otherwise, open the table, concatenate with the main
        table, and close the table just opened. */
    If( i == 1,
        mainDt = Open( "C:\" || myFiles[i] ),
        dt = Open( "C:\" || myFiles[i] );
        mainDt = mainDt << Concatenate(
                dt,
                Append to First Table
        );
        Close( dt, NoSave );
        Wait( 0 );
    )
);
```

```
/* Give the final table a name. */
mainDt << Set Name( "Concatenated Files" );
```

Note: To run this script, go to **support.sas.com/jumpintojmp** and select **Solution 5.16**. Copy and paste the code into a new Script window, and then select **Edit ▶ Run Script** to see the results. The code to create the tables listed here can be found in Solution 5.16.

Discussion 5.16:

At the end of each loop, the data table is closed. Because JMP considers the closing of a data table a system-related task, it is possible that the table is actually close at a later time than you expect. Because we are reassigning the global variable that represents a different data table in each iteration of the loop, it is necessary for JMP to close the data table before starting the next iteration. To ensure JMP has time to complete any system-related task, a **Wait** statement was added with an argument of zero. This tells JMP to pause until pending system-related tasks are completed. Further information about the **Wait** function can be found in the "Programming Functions" chapter of the *JMP Scripting Guide.*

Question 5.17:

I'm using a release of JMP prior to JMP 7. How can I open and concatenate multiple files that have the same format?

Solution 5.17:

Prior to JMP 7, concatenating tables always resulted in a new data table. This is because the **Append to First Table** option was not yet available. Therefore, the two data tables that make up the new concatenated data table must be closed within the **For** loop.

```
/* Create a list of all the files to be concatenated. */
myFiles = {"Fat Content.jmp", "Total Carbohydrates.jmp",
    "Nutrients.jmp"};
```

```
/* Loop through each file. */
For( i = 1, i <= N Items( myFiles ), i++,
    /* If the file is first in the list, open it.
       Otherwise, open the table, concatenate with the main
       table, and close the originals.  */
  If( i == 1,
      mainDt = Open( "C:\" || myFiles[i] ),
      dt = Open( "C:\" || myFiles[i] );
      tmp = mainDt;
      mainDt = mainDt << Concatenate( dt );
      Close( dt, NoSave );
      Close( tmp, NoSave );
      Wait( 0 );
  )
);
```

```
/* Give the final table a name. */
mainDt << Set Name( "Concatenated Files" );
```

Note: To run this script, go to **support.sas.com/jumpintojmp** and select **Solution 5.17**. Copy and paste the code into a new Script window, and then select **Edit ▶ Run Script** to see the results. The code to create the tables listed here can be found in Solution 5.17.

Discussion 5.17:

Notice that we assigned the *tmp* global variable to be a reference to *mainDt* before the concatenation. Then we re-assigned *mainDt* to represent the new concatenated table after the concatenation. This allowed us to easily close the two data tables that made up the concatenated data table. The code to create the tables listed here can be found in Solution 5.17.

Question 5.18:

How can I use a global variable that represents a list as the argument for **Mean** when creating a Summary table?

Solution 5.18:

Force evaluation of the global variable with the **Eval()** function:

```
/* Open the Big Class sample data table. */
dt = Open( "$SAMPLE_DATA/Big Class.JMP" );

/* Assign a global variable to represent the list. */
meanCols = dt << Get Column Names( Continuous );

/* Wrap the global variable in an Eval() function. */
dt << Summary(
    Group( :age, :sex ),
    Mean( Eval( meanCols ) )
);
```

Note: To run this script, go to **support.sas.com/jumpintojmp** and select **Solution 5.18**. Copy and paste the code into a new Script window, and then select **Edit ▶ Run Script** to see the results.

Discussion 5.18:

Cast the list variable as the argument for **Mean()**, and wrap the variable in an **Eval()** function to force evaluation before it is used in the Summary statement.

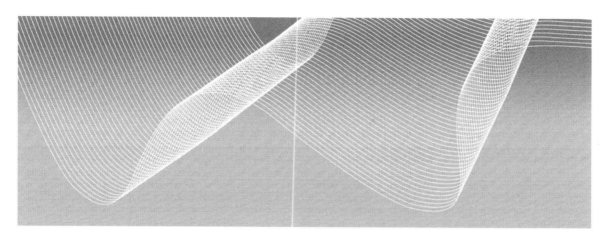

Chapter Six

Dialog Windows

Questions

Question 6.1:

How can I prompt the user to select a column to be used in an analysis?

Solution 6.1:

Use the **Column Dialog** command to present the user with a dialog window that includes all the columns in the data table as shown in the following code:

```
/* Open the sample data table, Big Class. */
dt = Open( "$SAMPLE_DATA/Big Class.jmp" );
```

```
/* Query the user for a single column. */
cdlg = Column Dialog(
   yCols = ColList( "Y, Response", MinCol( 1 ), MaxCol( 1 ) )
);

/* Unload the value from the Column Dialog */
my_Y = cdlg["yCols"];

/* Use the column value in an analysis.  This example uses the
   value in Distribution. */
dist = Distribution( Column( my_Y[1] ) );
```

Note: To run this script, go to **support.sas.com/jumpintojmp** and select **Solution 6.1**. Copy and paste the code into a new Script window, and then select **Edit ▶ Run Script** to see the results.

Discussion 6.1:

The value stored in the *yCols* variable inside the **Column Dialog** must be unloaded, as demonstrated previously, before it can be used in the analysis. More information regarding unloading values from a dialog window can be found in the "Modal Dialogs" section of the "Display Trees" chapter in the *JMP Scripting Guide*.

Result 6.1:

Figure 6.1 Column Dialog Window with One Column Selected

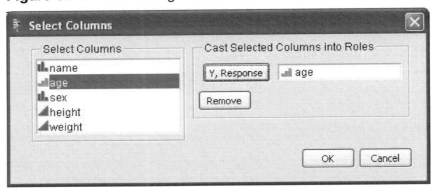

Figure 6.2 Distribution of Selected Column

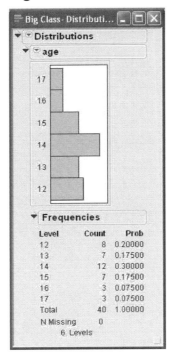

Question 6.2:

How can I stop a script if a user clicks the **Cancel** button in a dialog window?

Solution 6.2:

Create a dialog window to prompt the user for information. If **OK** is clicked, the value of *ageVar* is shown in the log. If **Cancel** is clicked, "Cancelled!" will be printed in the log and the script will stop.

```
/* Create a dialog to query the user. */
ageDlg = Dialog( "How old are you?",
        ageVar = EditNumber( 29 ),
        Button( "OK" ), Button( "Cancel" ) );

/* Test the result.  If -1, the Cancel button was clicked. */
If( ageDlg["button"] == -1,
  Print( "Cancelled!" );
  Throw();
);

/* Show variable result in log if OK was clicked. */
Show( ageDlg["ageVar"] );
```

Note: To run this script, go to **support.sas.com/jumpintojmp** and select **Solution 6.2**. Copy and paste the code into a new Script window, and then select **Edit ▶ Run Script** to see the results.

Discussion 6.2:

The **Throw()** function stops execution of the script. The last line of the example script demonstrates that the script stopped immediately after **Throw()** was invoked, as it is not executed when the user clicks the **Cancel** button.

Result 6.2:

Figure 6.3 Dialog Window Where Cancel Is Clicked

Dialog
How old are you?
29
OK
Cancel

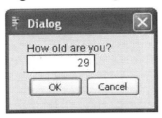

Figure 6.4 Log After Cancel Was Clicked

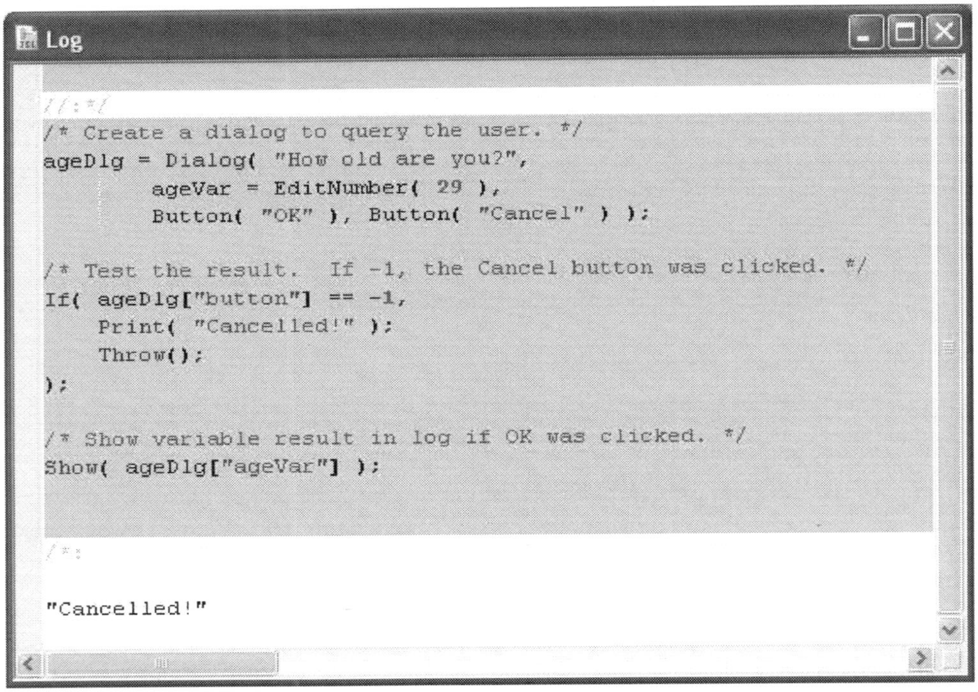

Log
//:*/
/* Create a dialog to query the user. */
ageDlg = Dialog("How old are you?",
ageVar = EditNumber(29),
Button("OK"), Button("Cancel"));
/* Test the result. If -1, the Cancel button was clicked. */
If(ageDlg["button"] == -1,
Print("Cancelled!");
Throw();
);
/* Show variable result in log if OK was clicked. */
Show(ageDlg["ageVar"]);
/*:
"Cancelled!"

Question 6.3:

How can I prompt the user to select a file in a specific directory? I want to display only those files of a specific type, such as Microsoft Excel.

Solution 6.3:

Use the **Pick File** command to specify the directory, and limit the file types displayed in the dialog window generated by the **Open** command as shown in the following code:

```
xlsFile = Pick File(
    "Select Excel File",
    "$SAMPLE_IMPORT_DATA",
    {"Excel Import Files | xls"}
);
```

```
/* Open the file the user selected and give it a reference. */
dt = Open( xlsFile );
```

Note: To run this script, go to **support.sas.com/jumpintojmp** and select **Solution 6.3**. Copy and paste the code into a new Script window, and then select **Edit ▶ Run Script** to see the results.

Discussion 6.3:

While **Pick File** initially became available with JMP 6, the options shown previously were added in JMP 7. More information about **Pick File** and its arguments can be found in the "Using the pick dialogs" section of the "Display Trees" chapter in the *JMP Scripting Guide*.

Result 6.3:

Figure 6.5 File Selection

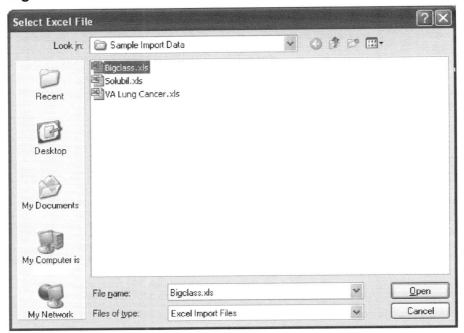

Question 6.4:

Can a wildcard character be used to open several data tables that contain specific characters in the filename?

Solution 6.4:

There are no available wildcard characters that can be used for opening files via JSL. Instead, you can use the **Pick Directory** function to prompt the user for a directory, extract the files using the **Files In Directory** function, and then loop through each item in the list of file names until all the files with the specified character string have been opened as shown in the following code:

```
/*  Prompt the user to select a directory.  For this example,
    we navigate to the following Windows directory:
 C:\Program Files\SAS\JMP\8\Support Files English\Sample Data
*/
path = Pick Directory( "Navigate to the directory where the
desired files are stored" );
```

```
/* Obtain a list of all the files in the directory. */
listOfFiles = Files In Directory( path );

/* Loop through each item in the list and remove the
   filename if it does not contain the specific characters. */
For( i = N Items( listOfFiles ), i >= 1, i--,
    If( !Contains( Uppercase( listOfFiles[i] ), "COMPARE" ),
        Remove From( listOfFiles, i )
    )
);
/*  Open each file in the list  */
For(k = 1, k<=Nitems(listOfFiles), k++,
  Open( path || listOfFiles[k] );
);
```

Note: To run this script, go to **support.sas.com/jumpintojmp** and select **Solution 6.4**. Copy and paste the code into a new Script window, and then select **Edit ▶ Run Script** to see the results.

Discussion 6.4:

In this example, all the files containing the word "COMPARE" in the filename will be included. Uppercase was used to ensure the case of the actual filename matches that of the search term, "COMPARE."

Result 6.4:

Figure 6.6 Pick Directory

Figure 6.7 Tables Opened That Contain "COMPARE" in the Filename

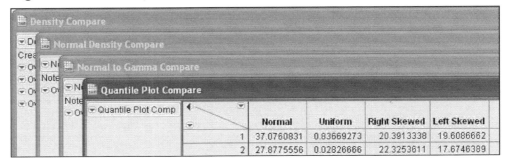

Question 6.5:

I am using JMP 6 and need to know how I can prompt the user for information, and then use that value in the SQL for extracting data from a database?

Solution 6.5:

Prompt the user for a value, then concatenate that value into the SQL string:

```
/* Prompt user for an age to be used in the SQL string. */
dlg = Dialog( "Enter Age",
   selAge = EditNumber( 12 ),
   Button( "OK" ), Button( "Cancel" )
);

/* Create a string that contains actual SQL concatenated
   with the user specified value from the dialog. */
sqlStr = "SELECT * FROM `Bigclass$` where age >= " ||
   Char( dlg["selAge"] );

/* Use the variable as the second argument. */
dt = Open Database( "Connect Dialog", sqlStr );
```

Note: To run this script, go to **support.sas.com/jumpintojmp** and select **Solution 6.5**. Copy and paste the code into a new Script window, and then select **Edit ▶ Run Script** to see the results.

Discussion 6.5:

In this example, the user is being prompted to enter an age. That age value is then used in the *sqlStr* string variable that is later used as the SQL query specified in second argument for the **Open Database** command.

Notice, the first argument in the **Open Database** command is listed as `Connect Dialog`. Normally, you would include the actual connection information. If you run this code, you will be prompted to select your Excel ODBC driver and then navigate to the appropriate Excel file. For this example, the intent is for you to open the Bigclass.xls file which is included as sample data in the following directory for a default installation on Windows:

C:\Program Files\SAS\JMP6\Support Files English\Sample Import Data

Detailed information regarding the **Open Database** command can be found in the "Database access (Windows and Linux only)" section of the "Production Environments" chapter in the *JMP Scripting Guide*. There is also helpful information in the "Connections: JMP and ODBC" white paper located on the JMP Web site:

www.jmp.com/software/whitepapers/

Result 6.5:

Figure 6.8 Dialog Window

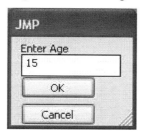

Figure 6.9 Select Excel Data Source

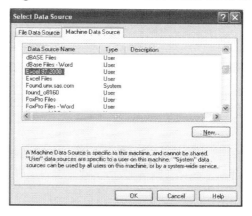

Figure 6.10 Select Excel File

Figure 6.11 Imported Data That Honored the User Selection

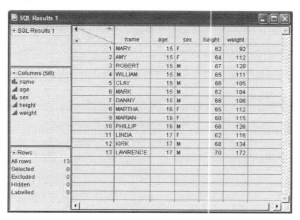

Question 6.6:

I am using JMP 7 or later. How can I prompt the user for information, and then use that value in the SQL for extracting data from a database?

Solution 6.6:

Prompt the user for a value, then place that value into the SQL string using **Eval Insert**():

```
/* Prompt user for an age to be used in the SQL. */
dlg = Dialog( "Enter Age",
   selAge = EditNumber( 12 ),
   Button( "OK" ), Button( "Cancel" )
);

/* Extract the value from the dialog. */
selAge = dlg["selAge"];

/* Create a string that contains actual SQL and wrap
   the global variable in carats (^). */
sqlStr = "SELECT * FROM `Bigclass$` where age >= ^selAge^";

/* Use the Eval Insert function to evaluate the global
   variable and use the SQL string as the second argument. */
dt = Open Database( "Connect Dialog", Eval Insert( sqlStr ) );
```

Note: To run this script, go to **support.sas.com/jumpintojmp** and select **Solution 6.6**. Copy and paste the code into a new Script window, and then select **Edit ▶ Run Script** to see the results.

Discussion 6.6:

In this example, the user is being prompted to enter an age. That age value is then used in the *sqlStr* string variable that is later used as the SQL query specified in second argument for the **Open Database** command.

Notice, the first argument to the **Open Database** command is listed as `Connect Dialog`. Typically, you would include the actual connection information. If you run this code, you will be prompted to select your Excel ODBC driver, and then navigate to the appropriate Excel file. For this example, the intent is for you to open the Bigclass.xls file, which is included as sample data in the following directory for a default installation on Windows:

C:\Program Files\SAS\JMP\8\Support Files English\Sample Import Data

Detailed information regarding the **Open Database** command can be found in the "Database access (Windows and Linux only)" section of the "Production Environments" chapter in the *JMP Scripting Guide*. There is also helpful information in the "Connections: JMP and ODBC" white paper, which is located on the JMP Web site:

www.jmp.com/software/whitepapers/

Result 6.6:

Figure 6.12 Dialog Window

Figure 6.13 Select Excel Data Source

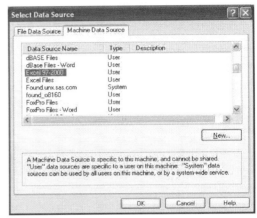

Figure 6.14 Select Excel File

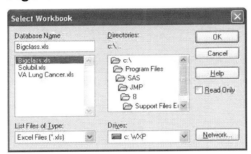

Figure 6.15 Imported Data That Honored the User Selection

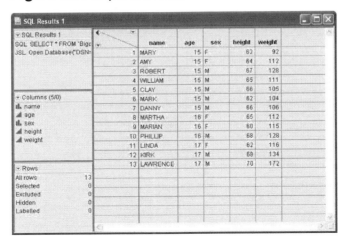

Question 6.7:

How can I prompt the user for information in a New Window, but simultaneously make JMP wait for the user input before going on to the next JSL statement?

Solution 6.7:

Create a flag variable to signal when the OK button has been clicked by the user:

```
/*  Create a flag that will be set when the user
    dismisses the window  */
while_flag = 0;

/*  New Window dialog  */
nw = New Window( "Roadrunner vs. Coyote",
    Outline Box( "Roadrunner vs. Coyote",
        H List Box( Text Box( "  Who always wins?  " ),
            tb = Text Edit Box( "?" )
        ),
        V List Box(
            Button Box( "OK",
                winner = tb << Get Text;
                while_flag = 1;       // Flag changes to 1
                nw << Close Window;
            )
        )
    )
);

/*  If while_flag is 0, JMP will wait  */
While( !while_flag, Wait( 0.1 ) );

/*  Evaluated only after while_flag has a value of 1  */
If( Uppercase( winner ) == "ROADRUNNER",
    Print( "You're a winner!" ),
    Print( "Thanks for playing. Please try again." )
);
```

Note: To run this script, go to **support.sas.com/jumpintojmp** and select **Solution 6.7**. Copy and paste the code into a new Script window, and then select **Edit ▶ Run Script** to see the results.

Discussion 6.7:

Because New Windows are non-modal, JMP will continue processing JSL commands unless you tell it to wait. This example demonstrates the use of a **While** command and a flag that gets set only when the user clicks a button in the window.

Result 6.7:

Figure 6.16 New Window

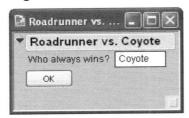

Figure 6.17 Log After Question Was Answered Incorrectly

```
    Outline Box( "Roadrunner vs. Coyote",
        H List Box( Text Box( "  Who always wins?  " ),
            tb = Text Edit Box( "?" )
        ),
        V List Box(
            Button Box( "OK",
                winner = tb << Get Text;
                while_flag = 1;       // Flag changes to 1
                nw << Close Window;
            )
        )
    )
);

/*  If while_flag is 0, JMP will wait  */
While( !while_flag, Wait( 0.1 ) );

/*  Evaluated only after while_flag has a value of 1  */
If( Uppercase( winner ) == "ROADRUNNER",
    Print( "You're a winner!" ),
    Print( "Thanks for playing. Please try again." )
);

/* :

"Thanks for playing. Please try again."
.
```

Question 6.8:

How can I populate a Combo Box based on a user selection of another combo box?

Solution 6.8:

Build the **New Window** using **Panel Boxes** and **Combo Boxes**, which will be dynamically populated based on user response.

```
/* Open the sample data table, Cars 1993. */
dt = Open( "$SAMPLE_DATA/Cars 1993.jmp" );

/* Create lists of the values found in the Manufacturer and
    Model columns. */
Summarize( autoMaker = By( Column( dt, "Manufacturer" ) ) );
Summarize( makeModel = By( Column( dt, "Model" ) ) );
```

```
/* Use New Window to create a non-modal dialog to display
    manufacturer and model for user to choose. */
nw = New Window( "Choose Models by Manufacturer",
    hb = H List Box(
        Panel Box( "Select a Manufacturer",
            select1 = Combo Box(
                autoMaker,
                /* Each of the following tasks are executed
                    when the user makes a Manufacturer choice.*/
                dt << Select Where(
                    :Manufacturer == autoMaker[select1 << get] );
                selRows = dt << Get Selected Rows;
                pb << delete;
                myModels = {};
                /* The myModels list is populated with values
                    from the selected manufacturer models. */
                For( i = 1, i <= N Row( selRows ), i++,
                    Insert Into( myModels,
                        Column( dt, "Model" )[selRows[i]] )
                );
                /* A new panel box is drawn and values shown
                    are based on manufacturer selection. */
                hb << Append( pb = Panel Box( "Select a Model",
                    select2 = Combo Box( myModels ) ) );
            )
        ),
        pb = Panel Box( "Choose a Model", Combo Box( " " ) )
    ),
```

```
        /* If user clicks OK, values displayed for manufacturer and
           model will be selected in table. */
        Button Box( "OK",
            nw << Close Window;
            dt << Select Where(
                :Manufacturer == autoMaker[select1 << get]
                &
                :Model == myModels[select2 << get]
            );
            /* Selected rows are subsetted into new table. */
            dt << Subset( Output Table Name( "Vehicle Details" ) );
        )
    );
```

Note: To run this script, go to **support.sas.com/jumpintojmp** and select **Solution 6.8**. Copy and paste the code into a new Script window, and then select **Edit ▶ Run Script** to see the results.

Discussion 6.8:

In this sample script, the user is being prompted to select a vehicle manufacturer. After that selection is made, JMP populates another **ComboBox** with the models produced by the selected manufacturer. Further, when the user clicks the **OK** button to dismiss the window, JMP produces a subset data table that contains the data for the selected manufacturer and model.

Result 6.8:

Figure 6.18 New Window Shows Only the Cadillac Models

Figure 6.19 Data Table Subset of Only Cadillac DeVille

		Manufacturer	Model	Vehicle Category	Minimum Price ($1000)	Midrange Price ($1000)	Maximum Price ($1000)
1		Cadillac	DeVille	Large	33	34.7	36.3

Vehicle Details
▼ Vehicle Details
Note Robin H. Lock, "1993 New C.
▼ Source
▼ Distribution
▼ Overlay Plot

Question 6.9:

I want to present the user with a list of columns in a dialog window that will
automatically generate a Distribution when they select the column name. How can this be
done?

Solution 6.9:

Build the New Window and ListBox and append the Distribution analysis based upon
user selection. The Distribution will remain live, so histogram bars can be clicked to
select rows in the data table.

```
/* Open the sample data table, Candy Bars. */
dt = Open( "$SAMPLE_DATA/Candy Bars.jmp" );
```

```
/* Obtain a list of column names which have a
   modeling type of Continuous. */
cols = dt << Get Column Names( Continuous );

/* Create a New Window to hold the ListBox of
   column names and the Distribution report. */
nw = New Window( "Test",
    hb = H List Box(
        Outline Box( "Select a column",
            /* Insert a ListBox containing the columns. */
            lb = List Box(
                cols,
                    /* Actions to be taken when a column is
                       selected in the ListBox. */
                    f = lb << Get Selected;
                    vb << Delete;
                    hb << Append(
                        vb = V List Box(
                            dist = dt << Distribution(
                                Continuous Distribution(
                                    Column( Eval( f[1] ) ) ),
                                Invisible
                            )
                        )
                    )
                )
            )
        ),
        vb = V List Box()
    )
);
```

Note: To run this script, go to **support.sas.com/jumpintojmp** and select **Solution 6.9**. Copy and paste the code into a new Script window, and then select **Edit ▶ Run Script** to see the results.

Result 6.9:

Figure 6.20 ListBox of Column Names

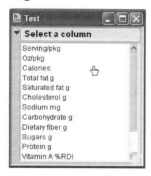

Figure 6.21 Live Distribution of Selected Column

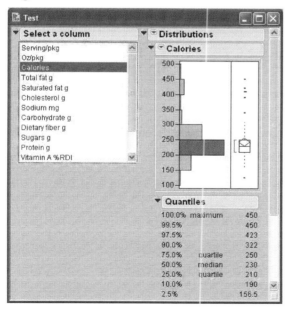

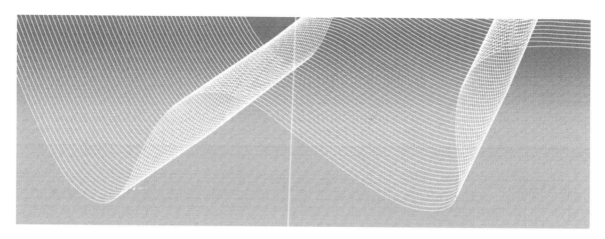

C h a p t e r   S e v e n

Analyses

Questions

Question 7.1:

How can I save the Parameter Estimates table from my Bivariate analysis into a new data table?

Solution 7.1:

Access the Parameter Estimates TableBox and send the **Make Into Data Table** message to create a data table with the values:

```
/* Open the Big Class sample data table. */
dt = Open( "$SAMPLE_DATA/Big Class.jmp" );

/* Generate the Bivariate analysis. */
biv = Bivariate(
        Y( :height ),
        X( :weight ),
        Fit Line
);

/* Create the new data table from the Parameter Estimates. */
Report( biv )["Parameter Estimates"][TableBox( 1 )] <<
                                    Make Into Data Table;
```

Note: To run this script, go to **support.sas.com/jumpintojmp** and select **Solution 7.1**. Copy and paste the code into a new Script window, and then select **Edit ▶ Run Script** to see the results.

Discussion 7.1:

How do you know which **TableBox** contains the data for the Parameter Estimates? First, open the Show Tree Structure window by right-clicking on the top-most blue disclosure triangle in the analysis window. (Note: If you are using a release prior to JMP 8, you will need to press the **CTRL+ SHIFT** keys while right-clicking the top-most blue disclosure triangle.) From the menu that appears, select **Edit ▶ Show Tree Structure**. After the Show Tree Structure window opens, locate the desired data (see Figure 7.1). In this case, the data is contained in the first **TableBox** under the "Parameter Estimates" OutlineBox.

Figure 7.1 Tree Structure of Parameter Estimates

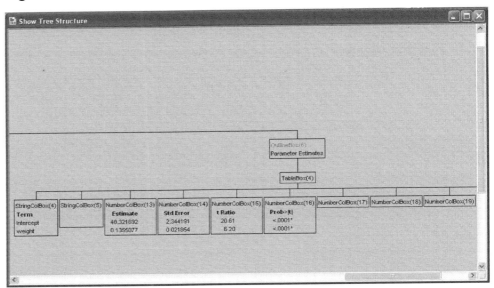

An alternative is to reference the exact display box and its number, as in the following example:

```
Report( biv )[TableBox( 4 )] << Make Into Data Table;
```

A drawback to this method is that it is a hard-coded value. As JMP evolves in the future, it is possible that the TableBox could change in a later release. In that case, your script would no longer produce the desired results.

Question 7.2:

How can I save the Parameter Estimates table from my Bivariate analysis into a new data table when I am using a By variable?

Solution 7.2:

Access a single Parameter Estimates TableBox and send the **Make Combined Data Table** message to create one data table with parameter estimate values from each By group report:

```
/* Open the Big Class sample data table. */
dt = Open( "$SAMPLE_DATA/Big Class.jmp" );

/* Generate the Bivariate using Age as the By variable. */
biv = Bivariate(
        Y( :height ),
        X( :weight ),
        Fit Line,
        By( :age )
);

/* Create the combined data table of Parameter Estimates. */
Report( biv[1] )["Parameter Estimates"][TableBox( 1 )] <<
                                Make Combined Data Table;
```

Note: To run this script, go to **support.sas.com/jumpintojmp** and select **Solution 7.2**. Copy and paste the code into a new Script window, and then select **Edit ▶ Run Script** to see the results.

Discussion 7.2:

How do you know which **TableBox** contains the data for the Parameter Estimates? First, open the Show Tree Structure window by right-clicking the top-most blue disclosure triangle in the analysis window. (Note: If you are using a release prior to JMP 8, you will need to press the **CTRL+ SHIFT** keys while right-clicking the top-most blue disclosure triangle.) From the menu that appears, select **Edit ▶ Show Tree Structure**. After the Show Tree Structure window opens, locate the desired data (see Figure 7.1). In this case, the data is contained in the first **TableBox** under the "Parameter Estimates" OutlineBox.

An alternative is to reference the exact TableBox and its number, as in the following example:

```
Report(biv[1])[TableBox(3)] << Make Combined Data Table;
```

A drawback to this method is that it is a hard-coded value. As JMP evolves in the future, it is possible that the **TableBox** could change in a later release. In this case, your script would no longer produce the desired results.

As discussed in Chapter Three, JMP provides a convenient method for making one table for all the related member nodes. Because *biv* represents a list of Bivariate analyses, we must use a subscript to identify a Bivariate analysis that we want to access. Note that the first Bivariate object is referenced as *biv[1]*. Sending the **Make Combined Data Table** message to only one member of the list will create a single table containing the data for all report tables of the same kind from throughout the report.

Note: The **Make Combined Date Table** option became available beginning with JMP 6.

Question 7.3:

I am using the Partition platform and need to click the **Split** button. How can I click the **Split** button from a JSL script?

Solution 7.3:

Send the **Click(1)** message to the Split Button Box:

```
/* Open the Mushroom sample data table. */
dt = Open( "$SAMPLE_DATA/Mushroom.jmp" );

/* Generate the Partition output. */
par = dt << Partition(
    Y( :Edibility ),
    X( :cap shape ),
    Split Best( 1 ),
    Criterion( Maximize Significance )
);
```

```
/* Click the Split button. */
Report( par )[Button Box( 1 )] << Click( 1 );
```

Note: To run this script, go to **support.sas.com/jumpintojmp** and select **Solution 7.3**. Copy and paste the code into a new Script window, and then select **Edit ▶ Run Script** to see the results.

Discussion 7.3:

This example demonstrates how the **Split** button of the Partition platform can be clicked from a script by sending the **Click(1)** message to the appropriate **ButtonBox**.

Result 7.3:

Figure 7.2 Partition Platform Report

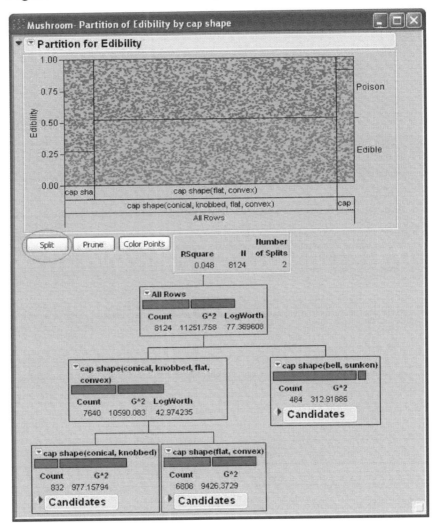

The **Click** message became available, beginning with JMP 7.

Question 7.4:

How do I use global variables for limit values in a Control Chart script?

Solution 7.4:

Initialize your global variables with limit values, and then (as appropriate) use these variables as arguments to LCL, UCL, and AVG as shown in the following code:

```
/* Open the sample data table, Pickles.jmp. */
dt = Open( "$SAMPLE_DATA/Quality Control/Pickles.jmp" );

/* Assign values to the limits global variables. */
upper = 14;
lower = 7;
average = 11;

/* Create Control Chart using the variable values. */
cc = dt << Control Chart(
    Sample Label( :Date ),
    K Sigma( 3 ),
    Chart Col( :Acid, Individual Measurement(
                UCL( upper ),
                AVG( average ),
                LCL( lower ) ) )
);
```

Note: To run this script, go to **support.sas.com/jumpintojmp** and select **Solution 7.4**. Copy and paste the code into a new Script window, and then select **Edit ▶ Run Script** to see the results.

Question 7.5:

For a control chart, how do I request JMP open and use a table of saved limits rather than those limits calculated at runtime?

Solution 7.5:

Use the **Get Limits()** option in the control chart platform object as shown in the following code:

```
/* Open the Pickles sample data table. */
dt = Open( "$SAMPLE_DATA/Quality Control/Pickles.jmp" );

/* Generate the Control Chart using the Get Limits option
   with the file path as the argument. */
cc = dt << Control Chart(
    Sample Label( :Date ),
    K Sigma( 3 ),
    Get Limits( "C:\LimitsTable.jmp" ),
    Chart Col( :Acid, Individual Measurement, Moving Range )
);
```

Note: To run this script, go to **support.sas.com/jumpintojmp** and select **Solution 7.5**. Copy and paste the code into a new Script window, and then select **Edit ▶ Run Script** to see the results. The code to create the LimitsTable.jmp file can be found in Solution 7.5.

Discussion 7.5:

The argument for the **Get Limits** option is the complete file path for the JMP table that contains the limits. The limits table will be opened in JMP when this option is used.

Question 7.6:

How do you save limits from the Control Chart analysis into the column property?

Solution 7.6:

Send the **Save Limits(In Column**) message to the Control Chart object, or include the option in the control chart platform command:

Option 1:

```
/* Open the Pickles sample data table. */
dt = Open( "$SAMPLE_DATA/Quality Control/Pickles.jmp" );

/* Generate the Control Chart. */
cc = dt << Control Chart(
  Sample Label( :Date ),
  K Sigma( 3 ),
  Chart Col( :Acid, Individual Measurement, Moving Range )
);

/* Save the limits in a new column. */
cc << Save Limits( In Column );
```

Option 2:

```
/* Open the Pickles sample data table. */
dt = Open( "$SAMPLE_DATA/Quality Control/Pickles.jmp" );

/* Generate the Control Chart using the Save Limits platform
   option with In Column as the argument. */
cc = dt << Control Chart(
  Sample Label( :Date ),
  K Sigma( 3 ),
  Save Limits( In Column ),
  Chart Col( :Acid, Individual Measurement, Moving Range )
);
```

Note: To run this script, go to **support.sas.com/jumpintojmp** and select **Solution 7.6**. Copy and paste the code into a new Script window, and then select **Edit ▶ Run Script** to see the results.

Discussion 7.6:

Option 1 demonstrates how to save the limits to the column property by sending the platform object reference a message. *Option 2* accomplishes the same goal but uses the option within the platform command instead. Specifying an option within a platform or sending a platform object reference a message are methods available in all platforms. For more information, see Chapter Three.

Result 7.6:

Limits have been saved to Control Limits column property of the process variable.

Figure 7.3 Saved Limits

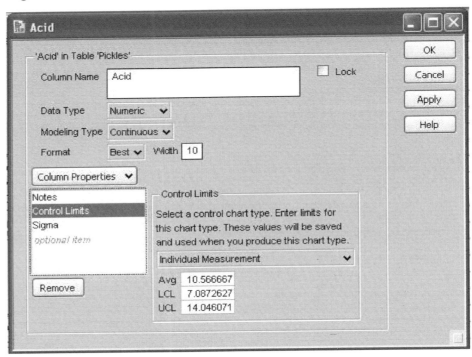

Question 7.7

How do you save limits from the Control Chart analysis into a new table?

Solution 7.7:

Send the **Save Limits** message to the platform reference using the **In New Table** argument as shown in the following code:

```
/* Open the Pickles sample data table. */
dt1 = Open( "$SAMPLE_DATA/Quality Control/Pickles.jmp" );

/* Generate the Control Chart. */
cc = dt1 << Control Chart(
    Sample Label( :Date ),
    Group Size( 1 ),
    KSigma( 3 ),
    Chart Col( :Acid, Individual Measurement, Moving Range )
);

/* Send Save Limits message to platform object. */
cc << Save Limits( In New Table );

/* Establish a reference to the new table. */
dt2 = Data Table( 1 );

/* Save the new table. */
dt2 << Save( "C:\LimitsTable.jmp" );
```

Note: To run this script, go to **support.sas.com/jumpintojmp** and select **Solution 7.7**. Copy and paste the code into a new Script window, and then select **Edit ▶ Run Script** to see the results.

Discussion 7.7:

The **Save Limits** option will place the limits into a new table. The rest of the code shows how to establish a reference to the table, and then how to save it.

Question 7.8:

How can I use spec limits stored in a separate data table?

Solution 7.8:

Obtain the spec limits stored in one data table, and assign the values to the Spec Limits column property of the desired column in the second table as shown in the following code:

```
/* Create a limits table for demonstration purposes. */
limitsDt = New Table( "Limits Table",
    Add Rows( 3 ),
    New Column( "Values", Numeric, Continuous,
        Format( "Best", 10 ), Set Values( [65, 50, 57] ) ),
    New Column( "Spec Limit", Character, Nominal,
        Set Values( {"Upper", "Lower", "Target"} ) )
);
```

```
/* Store the limits in global variables. */
lowerSpec = Column( limitsDt, "Values" )[2];
upperSpec = Column( limitsDt, "Values" )[1];
targetSpec = Column( limitsDt, "Values" )[3];
```

```
/* Open table where limits will be placed as a column
    property. */
dt = Open( "$SAMPLE_DATA/Big Class.jmp" );
```

```
/* Create an expression within an expression. */
specExpr = Expr(
    Column( dt, "height" ) << Set Property(
        "Spec Limits",
        {LSL( Expr( lowerSpec ) ),
        USL( Expr( upperSpec ) ),
        Target( Expr( targetSpec ) )}
    )
);
```

```
/* Resolve the global variable then evaluate the
    main expression. */
Eval( Eval Expr( specExpr ) );
```

```
/* Perform a distribution that demonstrates that the
    desired spec limits were used. */
```

```
dt << Distribution(
  Continuous Distribution(
      Column( :height )
  )
);
```

Note: To run this script, go to **support.sas.com/jumpintojmp** and select **Solution 7.8**. Copy and paste the code into a new Script window, and then select **Edit ▶ Run Script** to see the results.

Discussion 7.8:

Other options for spec limits can be found in a script titled "Managing Spec Limits with JMP," which was written by Ian Cox and is located in the JMP User Community File Exchange section:

www.jmp.com/community/

Question 7.9:

I have many variables in my data table and want to perform a Stepwise regression analysis, and then run my new model. How do I script this?

Solution 7.9:

Specify the limiting parameters in the **Run Model** arguments, and then send the **Finish** message to the platform object. A second Fit Model dialog window is created. Send the **Make Model** message to this dialog window as shown in the following code:

```
/* Open a sample data table for demonstration purposes. */
dt = Open( "$SAMPLE_DATA/Fitness.jmp" );

/* Launch the Fit Model platform. */
fit = dt << Fit Model(
    Y( :Oxy ),
    Effects( :Weight, :Runtime, :RunPulse, :RstPulse, :MaxPulse
),
    Personality( Stepwise ),
    Run Model( Prob to Enter( 0.2 ),
               Direction( Mixed ),
               Prob to Leave( 0.2 ) )
);

/* Force the stepwise to finish. */
fit << Finish;

/* Create the stepped model dialog. */
sm = fit << Make Model;

/* Execute the stepped model. */
sm << Run Model;
```

Note: To run this script, go to **support.sas.com/jumpintojmp** and select **Solution 7.9**. Copy and paste the code into a new Script window, and then select **Edit ▶ Run Script** to see the results.

Discussion 7.9:

To learn more about the options available for Stepwise Fit Model, go to **Help** ▶ **Indexes** ▶ **Object Scripting**. Browse to **Fit Stepwise** and select.

Question 7.10:

I need to close the Fit Model dialog window. How do I reference it?

Solution 7.10:

Use **Model Dialog**[n] as reference, where n refers to the number of the particular dialog window as shown in the following code:

```
Model Dialog[1] << Close Window;
```

Note: To run this script, go to **support.sas.com/jumpintojmp** and select **Solution 7.10**. Copy and paste the code into a new Script window, and then select **Edit ▶ Run Script** to see the results.

Discussion 7.10:

Here's a tip for when there is more than one Model Dialog window to be closed.

If you have two Model Dialog windows open, and you close the first one with this command:

```
Model Dialog[1] << Close Window;
```

Use the same command to close the second Model Dialog window, as there will be just one model dialog window left:

```
Model Dialog[1] << Close Window;
```

Question 7.11:

How can I use a list in place of the Fit Model effects?

Solution 7.11:

Build the Fit Model statement as an expression as shown in the following code:

```
/* Open the Big Class sample data table. */
dt = Open( "$SAMPLE_DATA/Big Class.JMP" );
```

```
/* Create the main expression with the response argument. */
myExpr = Expr( Fit Model( Y( :weight ) ) );

/* Build the effects expression. */
effectExpr = Expr( Effects() );

/* Assign a global variable to represent the list. */
myCols = {:age, :sex, :height};
For( i = 1, i <= N Items( myCols ), i++,
  Insert Into( effectExpr, myCols[i] )
);

/* Place the effectExpr into myExpr. */
Insert Into( myExpr, Name Expr( effectExpr ) );
Insert Into( myExpr, Expr( Personality(
                                    Standard Least Squares ) ) );

/* Insert the Run Model options into myExpr. */
Insert Into(
  myExpr,
  Expr(
      Run Model(
              :weight << {Plot Actual by Predicted( 1 ),
                          Plot Residual by Predicted( 1 ),
                          Plot Effect Leverage( 1 )}
      )
  )
);

/* Print expression to the log, for demonstration purposes. */
Show( Name Expr( myExpr ) );

/* Evaluate the expression. */
myExpr;
```

Note: To run this script, go to **support.sas.com/jumpintojmp** and select **Solution 7.11**. Copy and paste the code into a new Script window, and then select **Edit ▶ Run Script** to see the results.

Discussion 7.11:

The **Fit Model** expression is built in four steps:

1. Create *myExpr*, which is the main **Fit Model** expression, with the first argument.

2. Build the *effectExpr* by using a **For** loop to insert the elements of the column list into it.

3. Place the *effectExpr* inside the *myExpr* using the **InsertInto** function.

4. Insert the **RunModel** arguments into *myExpr*.

Question 7.12:

How do I save X number of principal components of my multivariate analysis to the data table? I also want to include the eigenvectors in my report and save them into a new data table.

Solution 7.12:

Nest the **Save Principal Components** and **Eigenvectors** options inside the **Principal Components** option for the multivariate analysis as shown in the following code:

```
/* Open the Solubility sample data table. */
dt = Open( "$SAMPLE_DATA/Solubility.jmp" );
```

```
/* Create multivariate analysis with Principal Components
    Arguments. */
mult = Multivariate(
    Y( :Name( "1-Octanol" ),
        :Ether,
        :Chloroform,
        :Benzene,
        :Carbon Tetrachloride,
        :Hexane ),
    Correlations Multivariate( 0 ),
    Principal Components( on Correlations,
                        Save Principal Components( 3 ),
                        Eigenvectors )
);

/* Send message to EigenVectors table to create a data table */
newDt = Report( mult )["Eigenvectors"][Table Box( 1 )]
                                << Make Into Data Table;

/* Name the new table. */
newDt << Set Name( "Eigenvectors" );
```

Note: To run this script, go to **support.sas.com/jumpintojmp** and select **Solution 7.12**. Copy and paste the code into a new Script window, and then select **Edit ▶ Run Script** to see the results.

Discussion 7.12:

Specify the number of principal components to be saved to the data table as the argument for **Save Principal Components**.

The **Eigenvectors** option became available beginning with JMP 7.

Question 7.13:

How can I save the Mahalanobis outlier, Jackknife distances, and T-square values of the outlier analysis to the data table?

Solution 7.13:

Set the options for each as shown in this code:

```
/* Open the sample data table, Solubility.jmp. */
dt = Open( "$SAMPLE_DATA/Solubility.jmp" );
```

```
/* Create multivariate analysis. */
mult = dt << Multivariate(
  Y( :Ether, :Name( "1-Octanol" ), :Carbon Tetrachloride,
      :Benzene, :Hexane, :Chloroform ),
  Estimation Method( "REML" ),
  Scatterplot Matrix( Density Ellipses( 1 ), Shaded Ellipses( 0
    ), Ellipse Color( 3 ) ),

  /* Set option for Mahalanobis and save values to table. */
  Mahalanobis Distances( 1, Save Outlier Distances( 1 ) ),

  /* Set option for Jackknife and save values to table. */
  Jackknife Distances( 1, Save Jackknife Distances( 1 ) ),

  /* Set option for T square and save values to table. */
  Tsquare( 1, Save Tsquare( 1 ) )
);
```

Note: To run this script, go to **support.sas.com/jumpintojmp** and select **Solution 7.13**. Copy and paste the code into a new Script window, and then select **Edit ▶ Run Script** to see the results.

Discussion 7.13:

Mahalanobis(1), **Jackknife(1)**, and **Tsquare(1)** are the messages to create these analyses in the multivariate report. To save the values that these reports generate as new columns in the data table, use the **Save** option nested within that argument.

You can use the terms Tsquare, T Square, or T², interchangeably.

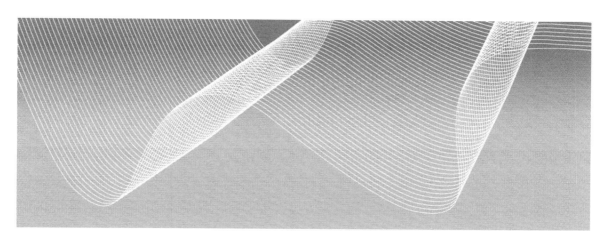

C h a p t e r   E i g h t

Graph Axes

Questions

Question 8.1:

How do I replace the default axis label with a different label?

Solution 8.1:

First, send a message to the **AxisBox** to remove the current label, and then send another message to add your custom label. This code sample shows how to change the label for each axis, X and Y:

```
/* Open the Big Class sample data table. */
dt = Open( "$SAMPLE_DATA/Big Class.jmp" );

/* Create the desired analysis. */
ov = dt << Overlay Plot( X( :height ),
                         Y( :weight ),
                         Separate Axes( 1 ) );

/* Remove and replace the Y axis label. */
Report( ov )[AxisBox( 1 )] << Remove Axis Label();
Report( ov )[AxisBox( 1 )] << Add Axis Label( "Class Weight" );

/* Remove and replace the X axis label. */
Report( ov )[AxisBox( 2 )] << Remove Axis Label();
Report( ov )[AxisBox( 2 )] << Add Axis Label( "Class Height" );
```

Note: To run this script, go to **support.sas.com/jumpintojmp** and select **Solution 8.1**. Copy and paste the code into a new Script window, and then select **Edit ▶ Run Script** to see the results.

Discussion 8.1:

The same concept can be applied for many other graphs, including Control Charts.

How do you know which **AxisBox** to address? First, open the Show Tree Structure window by right-clicking the top-most blue disclosure triangle in the analysis window. (Note: If you are using a release prior to JMP 8, you will need to press the **CTRL+ SHIFT** keys while right-clicking the top-most blue disclosure triangle.) From the menu that appears, select **Edit ▶ Show Tree Structure**. After the Show Tree Structure window opens, locate the desired data.

Figure 8.1 Show Tree Structure Window

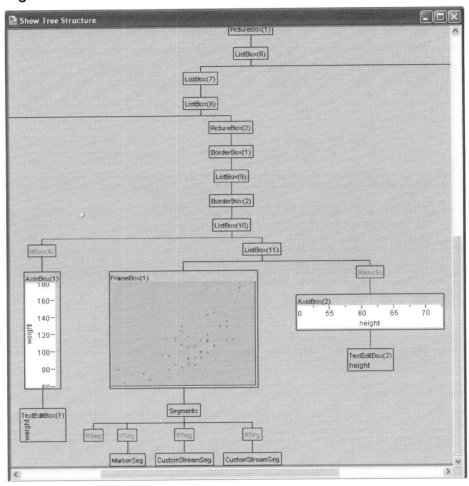

Question 8.2:

I have created an Overlay Plot with two Y axes. How do I replace all the default axis labels with different labels?

Solution 8.2:

Just as when there is only one Y axis, you first send a message to the **AxisBox** to remove the current label, and then send another message to add your custom label as shown in the following code:

```
/* Open the Big Class sample data table. */
dt = Open( "$SAMPLE_DATA/Big Class.jmp" );

/* Create the desired analysis. */
ov = dt << Overlay Plot(
          X( :age ),
          Y( :height, :weight ),
          Y Scale( Left, Right )
);
```

```
/* Remove and replace the axis labels. */
Report( ov )[Axisbox( 1 )] << Remove Axis Label();
Report( ov )[Axisbox( 1 )] << Add Axis Label( "Class Height" );
Report( ov )[Axisbox( 2 )] << Remove Axis Label();
Report( ov )[Axisbox( 2 )] << Add Axis Label( "Class Weight" );
Report( ov )[Axisbox( 3 )] << Remove Axis Label();
Report( ov )[Axisbox( 3 )] << Add Axis Label( "Class Age" );
```

Note: To run this script, go to **support.sas.com/jumpintojmp** and select **Solution 8.2**. Copy and paste the code into a new Script window, and then select **Edit ▶ Run Script** to see the results.

Discussion 8.2:

Notice the right Y axis will be **AxisBox (2)** and the X axis **AxisBox** becomes **AxisBox (3)**. To examine the **AxisBox** numbers, look at the Show Tree Structure window, which can be accessed by right-clicking the top-most blue disclosure triangle in the report window. (Note: If you are using a release prior to JMP 8, you will need to press the **CTRL+ SHIFT** keys while right-clicking the top-most blue disclosure triangle.) From the menu that appears, select **Edit ▶ Show Tree Structure**.

Question 8.3:

The font size, type, style, and color of the axis labels need to be changed. How do I accomplish this?

Solution 8.3:

Send messages to the appropriate **TextEditBox**, '1' for Y axis and '2' for X axis, to make the changes: **Set Font Size**, **Set Font Style**, **Font Color** as shown in the following code:

```
/* Open the Big Class sample data table. */
dt = Open( "$SAMPLE_DATA/Big Class.jmp" );

/* Create the desired analysis. */
ow = Oneway(
  Y( :height ),
  X( :sex ),
  Means( 1 ),
  Box Plots( 1 ),
  Mean Diamonds( 1 )
);
```

```
/* Y axis label is TextEditBox(1) in this example. */
Report( ow )[TextEditBox( 1 )] << Set Font Size( 14 );
Report( ow )[TextEditBox( 1 )] << Set Font( "Arial" );
Report( ow )[TextEditBox( 1 )] << Set Font Style( "Italic" );
Report( ow )[TextEditBox( 1 )] << Font Color( "Red" );

/* X axis label is TextEditBox(2) in this example. */
Report( ow )[TextEditBox( 2 )] << Set Font Size( 14 );
Report( ow )[TextEditBox( 2 )] << Set Font( "Arial" );
Report( ow )[TextEditBox( 2 )] << Set Font Style( "Italic" );
Report( ow )[TextEditBox( 2 )] << Font Color( "Red" );
```

Note: To run this script, go to **support.sas.com/jumpintojmp** and select **Solution 8.3**. Copy and paste the code into a new Script window, and then select **Edit ▶ Run Script** to see the results.

Discussion 8.3:

To determine which font sizes and font styles are available, go to **Help ▶ Indexes ▶ DisplayBox Scripting**, and then browse to **TextEditBox** and select **Set Font Style**, and **Set Font Size**.

For information on JMP colors, see the *JMP Scripting Guide*. To determine which fonts are available on your machine, right-click an axis, select the Axis Settings dialog window, and then click the **Font** button.

Figure 8.2 Axis Settings Font Window

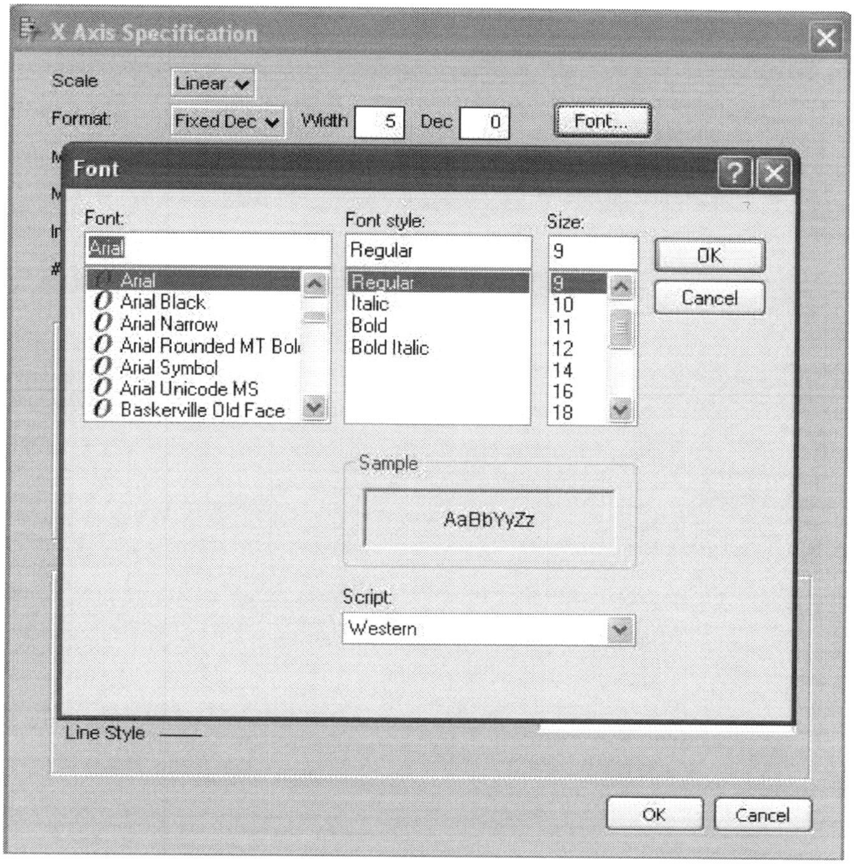

Question 8.4:

How do I specify a different font for the tick labels on my graph?

Solution 8.4:

Use the **Tick Font** message for the **AxisBox**, where you can specify **Style**, **Size**, and/or **Face** as the arguments as shown in the following code:

```
/* Open the Big Class sample data table. */
dt = Open( "$SAMPLE_DATA/Big Class.jmp" );

/* Create the desired analysis. */
ov = dt << Overlay Plot( X( :height ),
                         Y( :weight ),
                         Separate Axes( 1 ) );

/* Set the style, size, and face using Tick Font. */
Report( ov )[AxisBox( 1 )] << Tick Font( Style( 2 ),
                                         Size( 14 ),
                                         Face( "Arial Black" )
);
```

Note: To run this script, go to **support.sas.com/jumpintojmp** and select **Solution 8.4**. Copy and paste the code into a new Script window, and then select **Edit ▶ Run Script** to see the results.

Discussion 8.4:

The **Tick Font** option became available in JMP 7.

The font styles, sizes, and faces that are available on a machine can be determined interactively by right-clicking a plot axis, selecting the Axis Settings dialog window, and clicking the **Font** button (see Figure 8.2).

Question 8.5:

The tick labels on an axis need to be rotated and formatted to two decimal places. How is this done?

Solution 8.5:

Rotate the labels using the **Rotated Labels** message, and use the **Format** message to change the formatting of the labels. Both messages are sent to the AxisBox as shown in the following code:

```
/* Open the Big Class sample data table. */
dt = Open( "$SAMPLE_DATA/Big Class.jmp" );

/* Create the desired analysis. */
ov = dt << Overlay Plot( X( :height ),
                         Y( :weight ),
                         Separate Axes( 1 ) );

/* Rotate the axis labels. */
Report( ov )[AxisBox( 2 )] << Rotated Labels( 1 );

/* Set the axis label format to 2 decimal places. */
Report( ov )[AxisBox( 2 )] << Format( Fixed Dec, 4, 2 );
```

Note: To run this script, go to **support.sas.com/jumpintojmp** and select **Solution 8.5**. Copy and paste the code into a new Script window, and then select **Edit ▶ Run Script** to see the results.

Discussion 8.5:

The arguments for **Rotated Labels** are Boolean; use '1' for yes and '0' for no.

To see the available options for the **Format** function, right-click an axis, select the Axis Settings dialog window, and then click the down arrow for Format to display the list.

Figure 8.3 Axis Settings Format Menu

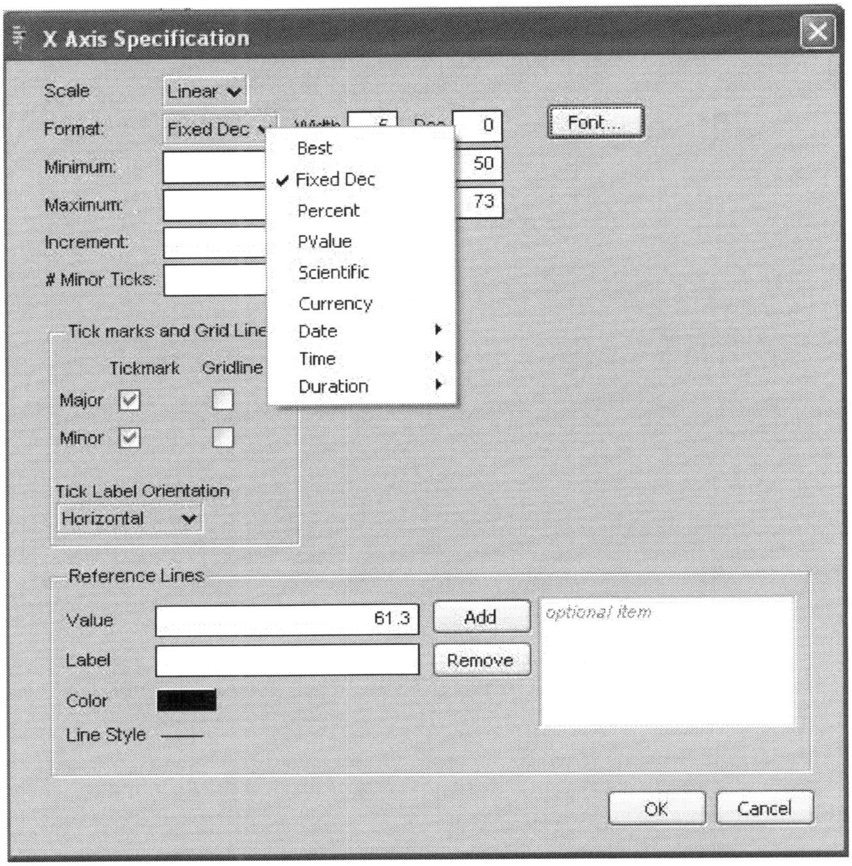

Question 8.6:

How can I specify the order of an axis?

Solution 8.6:

Assign the **Value Ordering** column property using the **Set Property()** message for the column as shown in the following code:

```
/* Open the Big Class sample data table. */
dt = Open( "$SAMPLE_DATA/Big Class.jmp" );
```

```
/* Assign the Value Ordering column property. */
Column( "age" ) << Set Property(
    Value Ordering,
    {17, 15, 16, 12, 13, 14}
);
```

```
/* Create a Bar Chart to see the effect. */
Chart( X( :age ), Y( Mean( :height ) ), Bar Chart( 1 ) );
```

Note: To run this script, go to **support.sas.com/jumpintojmp** and select **Solution 8.6**. Copy and paste the code into a new Script window, and then select **Edit ▶ Run Script** to see the results.

Result 8.6:

To check the Value Ordering property for the column, Age, right-click the column header, and then select **Column Info**.

Figure 8.4 New Value Ordering Property

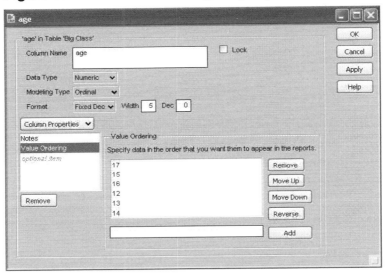

Figure 8.5 Bar Chart Demonstrates the New Axis Order

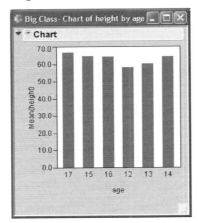

Question 8.7:

How can I use a global variable that represents a list to specify the order of an axis?

Solution 8.7:

Use the **Eval()** function to force evaluation of the global variable:

```
/* Open the Big Class sample data table. */
dt = Open( "$SAMPLE_DATA/Big Class.jmp" );

/* Assign a global variable to represent the list. */
myset = {17, 15, 16, 12, 13, 14};

/* Wrap the global variable in an Eval() function. */
Column( "age" ) << Set Property(
    Value Ordering,
    Eval( myset )
);

/* Create a Distribution to see the effect. */
Distribution( Nominal Distribution( Column( :age ) ) );
```

Note: To run this script, go to **support.sas.com/jumpintojmp** and select **Solution 8.7**. Copy and paste the code into a new Script window, and then select **Edit ▶ Run Script** to see the results.

Discussion 8.7:

The **Eval()** function forces evaluation of the list reference before it is used in the Set Property statement.

Result 8.7:

Figure 8.6 New Value Ordering Property

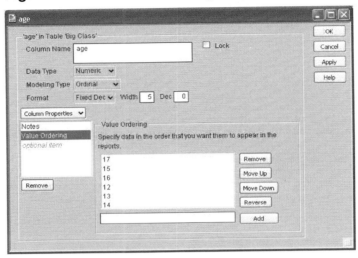

Figure 8.7 Distribution Demonstrates New Axis Order

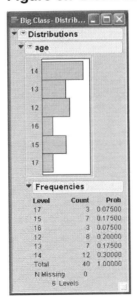

Question 8.8:

How do I add a reference line on any graph?

Solution 8.8:

Send an **Add Ref Line** message to the **AxisBox** as shown in the following code:

```
/* Open the Big Class sample data table. */
dt = Open( "$SAMPLE_DATA/Big Class.jmp" );

/* Create the desired analysis. */
ov = dt << Overlay Plot( X( :height ),
                         Y( :weight ),
                         Separate Axes( 1 ) );

/* Add a reference line to the Y axis. */
Report( ov )[Axisbox( 1 )] << Add Ref Line( 120, "Solid", "Red"
);

/* Add a reference line to the X axis. */
Report( ov )[Axisbox( 2 )] << Add Ref Line( 62.5, "Dashed",
"Green" );
```

Note: To run this script, go to **support.sas.com/jumpintojmp** and select **Solution 8.8**. Copy and paste the code into a new Script window, and then select **Edit ▶ Run Script** to see the results.

Discussion 8.8:

This example is for the Overlay Plot, but the concepts are the same for other graphs as well. The **Add Ref Line** message requires the number coordinate argument. Line style and color arguments might be included, as this example shows.

Question 8.9:

I am using JMP 8. How can I remove a reference line?

Solution 8.9:

Use the **Remove Ref Line** message as shown in the following code:

```
/* Open the Big Class sample data table. */
dt = Open( "$SAMPLE_DATA/Big Class.jmp" );

/* Create the desired analysis. */
ov = dt << Overlay Plot( X( :height ),
                         Y( :weight ),
                         Separate Axis( 1 ) );

/* Add a reference line to the Y axis. */
Report( ov )[AxisBox( 1 )] << Add Ref Line( 120,
                                            Solid,
                                            "Medium Dark Blue"
);

Wait( 2 );   /* Added for demonstration purposes only. */

/* Remove the reference line. */
Report( ov )[AxisBox( 1 )] << Remove Ref Line( 120 );
```

Note: To run this script, go to **support.sas.com/jumpintojmp** and select **Solution 8.9**. Copy and paste the code into a new Script window, and then select **Edit ▶ Run Script** to see the results.

Discussion 8.9:

The **Remove Ref Line** command was introduced in JMP 8.

Question 8.10:

I am using a version of JMP prior to JMP 8. How can I remove a reference line?

Solution 8.10:

Cover the current reference line with a similarly colored line:

```
/* Open the Big Class sample data table. */
dt = Open( "$SAMPLE_DATA/Big Class.jmp" );

/* Create the desired analysis. */
ov = dt << Overlay Plot( X( :height ),
                         Y( :weight ),
                         Separate Axis( 1 ) );

/* Add a reference line to the Y axis */
Report( ov )[AxisBox( 1 )] << Add Ref Line( 120 );

Wait( 2 );  /* Added for demonstration purposes only */

/* Cover the reference line with another that is a similar
   Color to the background. */
Report( ov )[AxisBox( 1 )] << Add Ref Line( 120,
                                            Solid,
                                            {255, 255, 250} );
```

Note: To run this script, go to **support.sas.com/jumpintojmp** and select **Solution 8.10**. Copy and paste the code into a new Script window, and then select **Edit ▶ Run Script** to see the results.

Discussion 8.10:

Prior to JMP 8, there was no JSL method for removing reference lines. As a workaround, you could add another reference line that is *nearly* the same color as the background. If you use the same color as the background, JMP will recognize that the colors are the same and will automatically change the color to something that is visible, which defeats the purpose of removing the line from view.

Question 8.11:

How do I add annotations to my graph using scripting?

Solution 8.11:

Use the **Text** function within **Add Graphics Script()** as shown in the following code:

```
/* Open the Big Class sample data table. */
dt = Open( "$SAMPLE_Data/Big Class.jmp" );

/* Generate the desired graph. */
cc = Control Chart(
  Sample Label( :age ),
  KSigma( 3 ),
  Chart Col( :height, Individual Measurement )
);
```

```
/* Use the Text function within Add Graphics Script()
   to add the desired text to the graph. */
Report( cc )[Framebox( 1 )] << Add Graphics Script(
  Text( right justified, {30, 55.0}, "ABC" );
  Text( right justified, {30, 70.0}, "XYZ" );
);
```

Note: To run this script, go to **support.sas.com/jumpintojmp** and select **Solution 8.11**. Copy and paste the code into a new Script window, and then select **Edit ▶ Run Script** to see the results.

Discussion 8.11:

The **Add Graphics Script** function enables running a script within a graph.

The *JMP Scripting Guide* and the "JSL Function Index" topic in the JMP Help provide information about the various options available for the **Text** function, including color, font, position, and orientation.

Question 8.12:

How can I change the line and marker attributes for each variable in my Overlay Plot?

Solution 8.12:

Specify line and marker attributes as shown in this code:

```
/* Open the Fitness sample data table. */
dt = Open( "$SAMPLE_DATA/Fitness.jmp" );

/* Create the desired analysis. */
op = dt << Overlay Plot( X( :Age ),
                         Y( :Weight, :Oxy, :Runtime ),
                         Y Scale( Left, Left, Right ),
                         Connect Thru Missing( 1 ) );

/* Added for demonstration purposes. */
Wait(0.5);
```

```
/* Change the properties of each legend item */
op << (weight(
    Overlay Marker( 3 ),
    Overlay Marker Color( Black ),
    Connect Color( Black ),
    Line Style( 1 ),
    Line Width( 2 )
));

/* Added for demonstration purposes. */
Wait(0.5);

op << (oxy(
    Overlay Marker( 6 ),
    Overlay Marker Color( Red ),
    Connect Color( Red ),
    Line Style( 4 ),
    Line Width( 1 )
));

/* Added for demonstration purposes. */
Wait(0.5);

op << (runtime(
    Overlay Marker( 1 ),
```

```
        Overlay Marker Color( Green ),
        Connect Color( Green ),
        Line Style( 0 ),
        Line Width( 1 )
));
```

Note: To run this script, go to **support.sas.com/jumpintojmp** and select **Solution 8.12**. Copy and paste the code into a new Script window, and then select **Edit ▶ Run Script** to see the results.

Discussion 8.12:

To change a line or marker attribute in an Overlay Plot, send the message to the platform object, with the particular attribute type nested in an expression that names the column name.

Color can be specified by a number in addition to the color name. For information about the number assignments for marker, color, and style, see the *JMP Scripting Guide*.

Result 8.12:

Figure 8.8 Overlay Plot

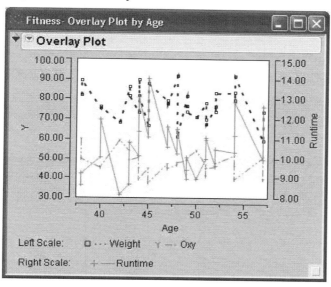

Question 8.13:

I have a spec limits table with columns holding limits for each process variable. I want to plot these limits on Oneway Plots. How can I do this?

Solution 8.13:

Use **Add Ref Line** to add lines to the plot, and as the argument to the command, use column and row references to the specific cell containing that information in the spec limits table as shown in the following code:

```
/* Open the sample data table, Big Class.jmp. */
dt1 = Open( "$SAMPLE_DATA/Big Class.jmp" );

/* For demonstration purposes, create a table with spec limits.
*/
dt2 = New Table( "Spec Limits Table",
  Add Rows( 2 ),
  New Column( "Process Column", Character, Nominal, Set Values(
{"height", "weight"} ) ),
  New Column( "Lower Spec Limit",
      Numeric,
      Continuous,
      Format( "Best", 10 ),
      Set Values( [60, 90] )
  ),
  New Column( "Upper Spec Limit",
      Numeric,
      Continuous,
      Format( "Best", 10 ),
      Set Values( [70, 150] )
  )
);

/* List of variables to be used in Oneway analyses. */
varList = {:height, :weight};
```

```
/* Use a For loop to create a Oneway ANOVA for each member of
   the variable list. */
For( i = 1, i <= N Items( varList ), i++,
  ow = dt1 << Oneway( Y( varList[i] ),
                X( :sex ),
                Means( 1 ),
                Box Plots( 0 ),
                Mean Diamonds( 1 ) );
```

```
/* Find the row in the data table that matches the column
   variable name. */
rownum = dt2 << Get Rows Where(
                :Process Column == Char( varList[i] ) );

/* Assign the limit value from adjacent columns on that row,
   using the rownum variable value. */
lower = Column( dt2, "Lower Spec Limit" )[rownum[1]];
upper = Column( dt2, "Upper Spec Limit" )[rownum[1]];

/* Add reference lines to the Oneway plot, based on the spec
   limit values assigned. */
Report( ow )[Axisbox( 1 )] << Add Ref Line(
                                    lower, Solid, Red );
Report( ow )[Axisbox( 1 )] << Add Ref Line(
                                    upper, Solid, Red );

);
```

Note: To run this script, go to **support.sas.com/jumpintojmp** and select **Solution 8.13**. Copy and paste the code into a new Script window, and then select **Edit ▶ Run Script** to see the results.

Result 8.13:

Figure 8.9 Oneway Plots with Limit Lines Added

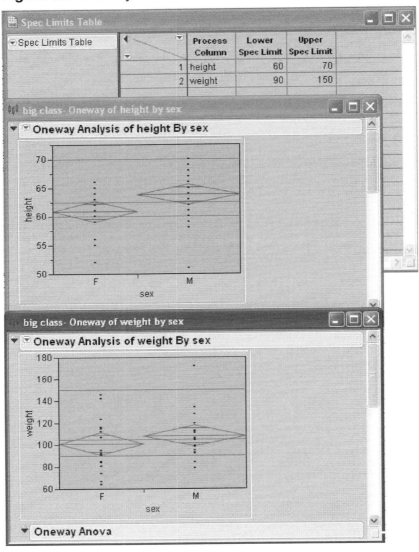

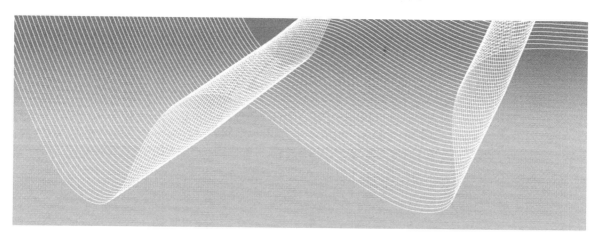

C h a p t e r   N i n e

Reports and Journals

Questions

Question 9.1:

At the top of my report, there is a text string that begins "Where…". How can I remove this information from my report?

Figure 9.1 Where String in Bivariate Report

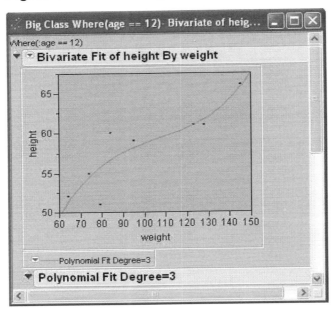

Solution 9.1:

Delete the **TextBox** above the topmost **OutlineBox** as shown in the following code:

```
/* Open the Big Class sample data table. */
dt = Open( "$SAMPLE_DATA/Big Class.jmp" );

/* Create a few Bivariate plots to demonstrate
   the Where text. */
For( i = 12, i <= 14, i++,
    biv = Bivariate(
        Y( :height ),
        X( :weight ),
        Where( :age == i ),
        Fit Polynomial( 3, {Line Color( "Green" ),
                            Line Style( Smooth )} )
    );
    Wait( 2 );  //For demonstration purposes.

    /* Delete the TextBox containing the Where text. */
    ( Report( biv ) << Parent )[Text Box( 1 )] << Delete;

    Wait( 2 );  //For demonstration purposes.
);
```

Note: To run this script, go to **support.sas.com/jumpintojmp** and select **Solution 9.1**. Copy and paste the code into a new Script window, and then select **Edit ▶ Run Script** to see the results.

Discussion 9.1:

The Where information appears as text above the **OutlineBox**. To access this **TextBox**, the **Parent** message is used to reference the text above the first **OutlineBox**. Finally, text can be removed by deleting the **TextBox**, as this example demonstrates.

The number associated with the **TextBox** is '1' in this case. However, if the Report Preferences have been set for "Date Title on Output" and/or "Data Table Title on Output", the **TextBox** number for the "Where" information might be '2' or '3'.

Because the **TextBox** appears above the uppermost blue disclosure icon, you cannot view the **TextBox** when viewing in the Show Tree Structure window.

More information about parent and child relationships within reports can be found in the *JMP Scripting Guide*.

Result 9.1:

Figure 9.2 Where Text Removed

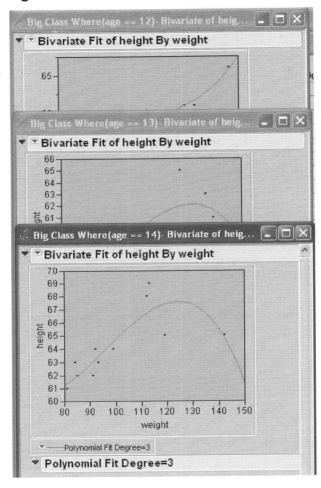

Question 9.2:

How can I use a variable in a Where statement so that the window title and Where text show the actual values rather than the variable name?

Solution 9.2:

Build an expression, then use **Eval Expr()** to resolve the global variable prior to evaluation of the expression:

```
/* Open the Fitness sample data table. */
dt = Open( "$SAMPLE_DATA/Fitness.jmp" );

/* Assign the criteria to a global variable. */
selVar = "M";
```

```
/* Build the main expression. */
bivExpr = Expr(
    Bivariate(
        Y( :MaxPulse ),
        X( :RstPulse ),
      /* Identify the global variable by wrapping it
         with the Expr function. */
        Where( :sex == Expr( selVar ) )
    )
);

/* Resolve the global variable expression first. Then
   resolve the main expression. */
Eval( Eval Expr( bivExpr ) );
```

Note: To run this script, go to **support.sas.com/jumpintojmp** and select **Solution 9.2**. Copy and paste the code into a new Script window, and then select **Edit ▶ Run Script** to see the results.

Discussion 9.2:

This solution illustrates how to use a global variable that contains a string, and how to place it in a **Where** clause in an analysis launch. First, an expression is built that contains a **Where** clause, which itself contains an expression.

In the last line of code, the **Eval Expr** function evaluates the **Expr(** *selVar* **)** within the main expression, *bivExpr*. Finally, the **Eval** function evaluates the main expression, *bivExpr*.

Question 9.3:

How can I arrange my Overlay Plot so that I have three graphs per row?

Solution 9.3:

The Overlay Plot provides an option called **Arrange Plots**, which enables you to place a specified number of plots per row as shown in the following code:

```
/* Open the Big Class sample data table. */
dt = Open( "$SAMPLE_DATA/Big Class.jmp" );
```

```
/* Create the Overlay Plot and include the Arrange Plots
    option. */
Overlay Plot(
    X( :weight ),
    Y( :height ),
    Grouping( :age ),
    Arrange Plots( 3 ),
    Connect Points( 1 ),
    By( :sex )
);
```

Note: To run this script, go to **support.sas.com/jumpintojmp** and select **Solution 9.3**. Copy and paste the code into a new Script window, and then select **Edit ▶ Run Script** to see the results.

Discussion 9.3:

The **Arrange Plots** option allows a numeric argument, which can be up to the number of levels in the grouping variable. If there is no grouping variable, the **Arrange Plots** option will be ignored.

Question 9.4:

How can I arrange my report so that I have two graphs per row?

Solution 9.4:

In most platforms, like this Bivariate example, it is possible to accomplish the task by appending reports for each level of the By variable into a **New Window** as shown in the following code:

```
/* Open the Big Class sample data table. */
dt = Open( "$SAMPLE_DATA/Big Class.jmp" );

/* Capture a list of each level of the By variable. */
Summarize( ageLevs = By( :age ) );

/* Determine the number of rows needed by dividing the
   number of levels in the By variable by the desired
   number of graphs per row. */
numLev = Ceiling( N Items( ageLevs ) / 2 );

/* Create an empty window where the graphs will be placed. */
New Window( "Bivariate by Age", vb = V List Box() );
```

```
/* Start a count at zero. */
ct = 0;
/* Loop through the number of rows needed. */
For( l = 1, l <= numLev, l++,
    /* Create an empty HListBox that will hold a single row of
       graphs. */
    hb = H List Box();
    /* Loop through the desired number of graphs per row. */
    For( i = 1, i <= 2, i++,
        /* Proceed as long as the count does not exceed the
           number levels of the By variable. */
        If( ct + i <= N Items( ageLevs ),
          /* Create the Bivariate for each By variable. */
            biv = Bivariate(
                Y( :weight ),
                X( :height ),
                Fit Line( {Line Color( "Red" )} ),
                Where( :age == Num( ageLevs [ct + i] ) ),
                Invisible
            );
            /* Set the title of the OutlineBox to show the
               correct By variable level. */
```

```
                    Report( biv )[Outline Box( 1 )] <<
                                    Set Title( ageLevs[ct + i] );
                    /* Append the report to the HListBox. */
                    hb << Append( Report( biv )[Outline Box( 1 )] <<
                                                Clone Box );

                    /* Close the Bivariate. */
                    biv << Close Window;
            )
        );
        /* Append the HListBox to the VListBox contained in the
           New Window. */
        vb << Append( hb );
        /* Increment the count by 2. */
        ct += 2;
    );
```

Note: To run this script, go to **support.sas.com/jumpintojmp** and select **Solution 9.4**. Copy and paste the code into a new Script window, and then select **Edit ▶ Run Script** to see the results.

Discussion 9.4:

VListBox and **HListBox** are Display Box constructors that aid in the spatial arrangement of reports and **New Windows**, where V is an abbreviation for vertical and H is an abbreviation for horizontal.

The sample demonstrates how to loop through each level of the By variable, create the Bivariate report, and place two graphs on each row. If there were an uneven number of levels, the last row would contain a single graph.

After the individual Bivariate reports are appended to a **HListBox**, the **HListBox** is then appended to the **VListBox**, which is part of the **New Window**.

Result 9.4:

Figure 9.3 Bivariate Reports Arranged Two Graphs per Row

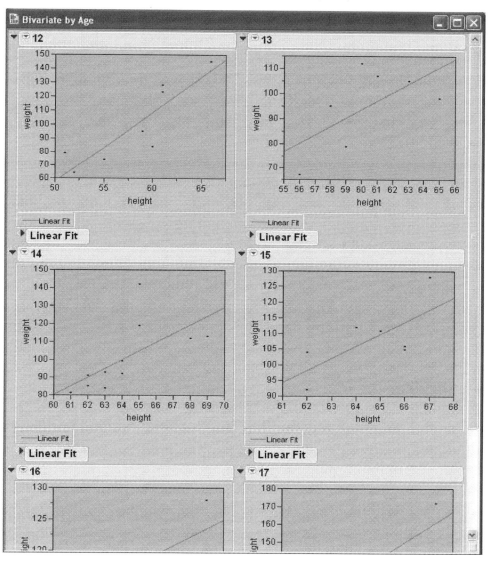

Question 9.5:

How can I get a handle to the journal window so that I can save it?

Solution 9.5:

Use the **Current Journal()** command as shown in the following code:

```
/* Open the Big Class sample data table. */
dt = Open( "$SAMPLE_DATA/Big Class.jmp" );

/* Generate the desired analysis. */
biv = dt << Bivariate( Y( :weight ), X( :height ), Fit Line );

/* Create a journal of the report. */
Report( biv ) << Journal;

/* Obtain a handle to the current journal. */
jrn = Current Journal();

/* Save the journal. */
jrn << Save Journal( "C:\DistJournal.jrn" );
```

Note: To run this script, go to **support.sas.com/jumpintojmp** and select **Solution 9.5**. Copy and paste the code into a new Script window, and then select **Edit ▶ Run Script** to see the results.

Discussion 9.5:

The **Current Journal** command became available in JMP 6. This command returns a reference to the active journal that is open in the JMP application.

Question 9.6:

How can I change the name of the journal window?

Solution 9.6:

Use **Set Window Title** to set the title to the journal window as shown in the following code:

```
/* Open the Big Class sample data table. */
dt = Open( "$SAMPLE_DATA/Big Class.jmp" );

/* Generate the desired analysis. */
biv = dt << Bivariate( Y( :weight ), X( :height ), Fit Line );

/* Create a journal of the report. */
Report(biv) << Journal;

/* Set the title of the journal window. */
Current Journal() << Set Window Title( "My New Journal" );
```

Note: To run this script, go to **support.sas.com/jumpintojmp** and select **Solution 9.6**. Copy and paste the code into a new Script window, and then select **Edit ▶ Run Script** to see the results.

Discussion 9.6:

The **Set Window Title** command can be used to change any window titles.

Question 9.7:

How do I insert the contents of a data table into a journal, under a specific OutlineBox?

Solution 9.7:

The example shows how to insert the sample data table, Big Class, under the Summary of Fit **OutlineBox** in a journal that contains a Bivariate report as shown in the following code:

```
/* Open the Big Class sample data table. */
dt = Open( "$SAMPLE_DATA/Big Class.jmp" );

/* Generate the desired analysis. */
biv = dt << Bivariate( Y( :weight ), X( :height ), Fit Line );

/* Create a journal of the report. */
Report( biv ) << Journal;

/* Obtain a handle to the current journal. */
jrn = Current Journal();

/* Save and close the journal. */
jrn << Save Journal( "C:\Bivariate.jrn" );
jrn << Close Window;

/* Journal the data table. */
dt << Journal;

/* Obtain a handle to the active journal. */
dt_jrn = Current Journal();

/* Get a script of journal. */
contents = dt_jrn << Get Journal();

/* Close the journaled table. */
dt_jrn << Close Window();

/* Put journal script into JournalBox constructor. */
jbox = Journal Box( contents );

/* Open saved journal of Bivariate report. */
jrn = Open( "C:\Bivariate.jrn" );

/* Insert an OutlineBox containing the JournalBox under the
   Summary of Fit table. */
```

```
Current Journal()["Summary of Fit"] << Append(
                          Outline Box( "Data Table", jbox ) );
```

Note: To run this script, go to **support.sas.com/jumpintojmp** and select **Solution 9.7**. Copy and paste the code into a new Script window, and then select **Edit ▶ Run Script** to see the results.

Discussion 9.7:

The JournalBox constructor will hold the journal text extracted from the journal file via **Get Journal()**. To append the JournalBox under a particular OutlineBox in the main journal, send the **Append** message to that OutlineBox.

Note: This script does not run correctly in JMP 8.0. Fortunately, the issue has been fixed in the JMP 8.0.1 maintenance release.

Result 9.7:

Figure 9.4 Journal with Data Table Inserted

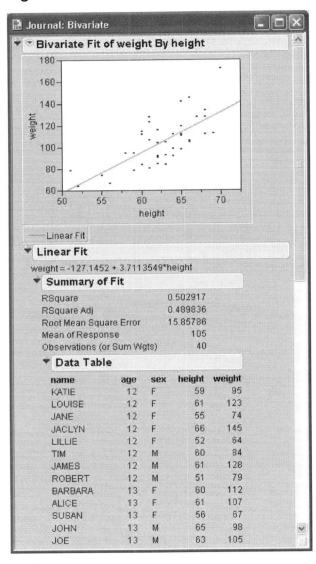

Index

25281805R00136

Made in the USA
Charleston, SC
19 December 2013